HOW TO PRAY

HOW TO PRAY

The chapters on prayer from *The School of Jesus Christ*

by

JEAN-NICOLAS GROU
of the Society of Jesus

translated by

JOSEPH DALBY, D.D.

JAMES CLARKE & CO. LTD.
5 Wardrobe Place, Carter Lane
London, E.C.4

This translation first published 1955

PRINTED IN GREAT BRITAIN
BY LATIMER, TREND AND CO. LTD.
PLYMOUTH

INTRODUCTION

Jean Nicolas Grou was born in 1730. He went to school with the Jesuits, became a novice and is next heard of as a teacher in the Jesuit College at La Flèche. His work gained a considerable reputation and he found time to translate several volumes of Plato's dialogues, which won high praise from the scholars of his day and were reprinted again and again. The suppression of the Jesuit Order brought him into trouble, but in 1766 we find him at Paris, whither he had come on the invitation of the Archbishop, living under the assumed name of Le Claire. His stay in Paris was a short one, but it was to mean much for him, for there he became acquainted with Mère Pélagie, a Visitation nun of great sanctity, who advised him to make the retreat which was the occasion of what he always called his conversion. This happened in 1767 or 1768, and thenceforward he becomes one of that band of saints who live their lives in the spirit of prayer, with a habitual sense of God's presence and complete abandon to his holy will. Later he goes to Holland where he is to remain for some years and does not return to Paris till 1776, where for some years he gives his time to the writings of books on the spiritual life. He produced two volumes of comments on St. Augustine's Confessions which later appeared in English under the title, *Morality Extracted from the Confessions of Saint Austin*. Amongst other writings there appeared later the *Maximes Spirituelles*. These maxims, twenty-four in number, are set out shortly in verse "that they may be grasped and retained more easily by the memory". A hundred years later John Mason Neale translated them into English and comments thus: Widely differing from the ordinary Jesuit teaching of the present day the spirit of Père Grou is almost identical with that embodied in our sound old English ascetic books such as *The Scale of Perfection*, *Holy Wisdom*, etc. At this period Père Grou was much occupied in giving addresses to various religious houses in Paris which were to be published in the book called *Manuel des Ames Intérieures*, perhaps the best known of all Père Grou's works and now published in English as the *Manual for Interior Souls*. It seems to be the basis also of a once well-known little book by H. L. Sydney Lear, *The Hidden Life of the Soul*.

Besides such work as this, a good deal of time was being given to the collection of materials for a work, *Traité dogmatic de la vraie religion*, undertaken at the request of the Archbishop. The manuscript, fruit of fourteen years' labour, got into the hands of a French priest who produced an unauthorized mangled edition under his own name, and it was only in 1792 that the author got it back into his own hands. As he was fleeing from France, he entrusted it to a lady who was arrested during the Terror; and her servants, thinking the manuscript might compromise her, deliberately burnt it. Later on Père Grou heard of the tragedy and made the characteristic comment: "If God wished to derive glory from that work he would have preserved it; since he has allowed it to perish he can as well make use of another for his purpose as of me."

The outbreak of the Revolution changed the whole course of Père Grou's life. He had been living a happy and peaceful life in Paris, his writings and preachings were widely known and greatly esteemed, and his work had been recognized by the bestowal of a pension by Louis XVI. His first thought was to stay in Paris and carry on his priestly work there secretly, but Mère Pélagie, herself a fugitive, wrote to him from her hiding-place in 1792, strongly urging him to fly from Paris. He knew nobody in England but Father Alexander Mackenzie, who had published translations of two of his works and was chaplain to a certain Mr. Thomas Weld of Lulworth Castle. As it happened, he received at this very time an invitation from Father Mackenzie asking him to come to him.

So it came about that Père Grou spent the last eleven years of his life in England at the house of a pious and munificent Roman Catholic layman. Thomas Weld was the father of a large family of children, many of whom came under Père Grou's influence, and his numerous benefactions made him the father of a far larger family of religious communities who looked to him as their patron or founder. We need only mention here that his mansion at Stonyhurst, Lancashire, was placed at the disposal of the exiled Jesuits from Liège. A disastrous fire has left Lulworth Castle a mere shell so that the little cell where Père Grou lived, scarcely larger than a big cupboard, can no longer be seen. He was greatly loved by the family, but he chose to live the life of a hermit in his little room, rising at four each morning, winter and summer, and spending his time in prayer and writing. We are told that in order to observe his vow of poverty he would not receive from his host any regular allowance, but would ask for food, clothing or books, just as the need arose. He regarded his solitary life as a special blessing given him by God. "Nothing", he writes in a letter, "is more opposed to my inclination than intercourse with mankind, and no motive but the glory of God and the salvation of my neighbour makes me engage in it. I love solitude, silence, work. I would rather be alone even with nothing to do, than take part in brilliant conversation in which I find nothing to interest me any more than in other things that belong to this lower world." Thus, whilst the old world of France was in ruins and Europe wracked with war, Père Grou lived the life of prayer and wrote his books. "I write nothing of myself", he said; "upon matters spiritual, God guides my pen. When I take it up I do not know what I am going to write and I am the first to be surprised at the thoughts which come to me." Père Cadrès who, examined all his MSS., says that, although some are known to have been composed very rapidly, they show no signs of correction or alteration, but seem "to have flowed from his pen without effort like water from a jet".

The last two years of his life were years of great suffering, but he would make no change in his way of life, or reduce the time given to his religious exercises. He died on 12th December 1803, in great peace. Almost at the beginning of this period of suffering he had received a great and unexpected consolation. He had always lived strictly the Jesuit life, even after the suppression of the Society, but now in 1801 the Pope gave his canonical approval to the Society in England, and so a few months before his death he was able to renew the the four vows of his solemn profession and to call himself openly a member of the Society of Jesus.

The School of Jesus Christ is in many ways the most important of all Père Grou's books, a full-dress treatise on the Christian life. Written during those last years in England, it is the ripe fruit of the author's life of prayer and meditation. The chapters on prayer form the first half of the second book, about a quarter of the whole work; they form in themselves a complete and independent treatise on Christian prayer. Evelyn Underhill, in one of her published letters, refers to them as "one of the best short expositions of the essence of prayer which has ever been written". The first chapters deal at length with the first consideration of all: we do not pray of ourselves, we cannot, it is God who teaches us to pray. Not that he teaches us in any external way as giving us instructions which we are to follow by ourselves. God teaches us to pray in an interior way, i.e. he inspires our prayers, so that we can say that all true prayer is God's prayer. Again and again Père Grou analyses the prayers that Christians make, probing into our motives and ruthlessly casting on one side all prayer that is not real prayer, i.e. prayer inspired by the Holy Spirit. It is not we who pray, but God who prays in us. Then follow four chapters on different aspects of prayer and it is not long before the author is giving us the very heart of his message and recommending the prayer of silence. "After stating our needs simply by word of mouth, if we prefer it, our Saviour bids us keep silence and allow our hearts to speak far more eloquently than our lips." The chapter on Continual Prayer reveals the massive common-sense of this hermit, for whilst he insists that we must pray without ceasing, he allows that prayer goes on through our actions and certainly through our sufferings; it can go on through our social duties and make us "more accessible, more genial and more obliging". In the chapter on Common Prayer he deliberately omits all consideration of public worship to deal entirely with household prayers. Here, more than anywhere else, we see the priest of the old régime for whom the patriarchal system of eighteenth-century France is a sacred ordinance. The whole is rounded off by the long chapter on the Lord's Prayer as the type and model of all prayer. As the prayer is expounded clause by clause, so carefully and lovingly, it is as though the author is writing in the very presence of the Lord who gave it.

The great French school of devotional writers which begins with St. Francis de Sales, has in recent years been introduced to English readers by the publication of the works of de Caussade, Grou and others. Of this school was also Baron von Hugel, for like Charles de Foucauld he was a pupil of the Abbé Huvelin. Evelyn Underhill finds the characteristic mark of these great French teachers in a twofold realism, i.e. there is on the one hand a vivid sense of the presence and transcendence of God, and on the other hand an acceptance of human nature as it really is, in all its limitations and many weaknesses. The human soul therefore must know its own nothingness, it must accept the fact of the human situation, abandoning itself to God with no reservations. And yet this abandonment of the soul is the very opposite of the fanatic's surrender, for it is to be completely homely and truly natural, the surrender of the tiny child to the parent's loving care.

Within this company of great masters of the spiritual life Père Grou has his own particular place. Abbot Butler said of him that he was "more gripping" than any other spiritual writer, "very ingoing, very exacting, but full of saving reasonableness". There is in him a strictness and austerity; you feel, when you read his words, that here is a man who did not spare himself and will not spare you, as long as you try to evade God's claims. It is true that the modern reader has to remind himself continually of the setting in which he wrote, that old authoritarian age which seems so far away. But if he will cross that line of division between Père Grou's world and his own he will be greatly rewarded. He will find a solidity, a thoroughness, strangely absent from so much devotional literature, he will be in touch with a great genius in the art of prayer who speaks only of what he practises himself. Père Grou was a truly inspired writer, for he wrote at God's command and as God gave him the words. His words will therefore endure.

J. D.

TRANSLATOR'S NOTE

This book is a reissue of a book under the same title published in 1898, but the translation has been freshly done from the French edition of Father Doyotte. I have reverted to the ancient custom of using small capitals for the personal pronoun when it refers to the Deity, which indeed is Grou's usage. I wish to acknowledge my indebtedness to Dom Huddleston's introduction to the English edition of *The School of Jesus Christ* for the brief sketch of Père Grou's life.

J. D.

CONTENTS

	Introduction	5
	Translator's Note	11
I.	*God Alone Teaches Us to Pray*	15
II.	*God Alone Teaches Us to Pray*	24
III.	*God Alone Teaches Us to Pray*	34
IV.	*God Alone Teaches Us to Pray*	44
V.	*God Alone Teaches Us to Pray*	53
VI.	*The Multiplicity of Vocal Prayers*	63
VII.	*The Efficacy of Prayer*	71
VIII.	*Continual Prayer*	79
IX.	*Common Prayer*	89
X.	*The Lord's Prayer*	99

CHAPTER I

GOD ALONE TEACHES US TO PRAY

One day the Apostles said to Jesus Christ: *Lord, teach us to pray*. It was the Holy Spirit who inspired them to make this request and at the same time gave them a most exalted idea of prayer, by means of which the creature draws near to God, adores him, gives him thanks, asks his forgiveness for its sins, and lays before him its needs. Filling them with a sense of their own nothingness and of God's greatness, the Holy Spirit convinced them of their inability in their own strength to attain to such excellent acts, and he moved their hearts to draw near to Jesus Christ, as the only Master who could teach them how they ought to pray and by his grace help them to do so. It was then that Jesus taught them the Dominical Prayer. We will study this later on.

There is no Christian who is not in the same case as the Apostles and who ought not to say to the Saviour as humbly as they: *Lord, teach us to pray*. Ah! if we were only convinced of our ignorance on this great subject and of our need of a Master like Jesus Christ! If we would only approach him with confidence, beseeching him to teach us himself and desiring to be taught by his grace in the science of conversing with God! How soon we should be skilled in it and how many of its secrets we should discover. Do not let us say that in teaching the Apostles he taught us and that we know the prayer they learnt from him. We know the words, but without grace we cannot understand the meaning and we cannot ask or obtain what it expresses. We have been outwardly taught as the disciples were when the Saviour answered their desire, but that is not enough. Like them we must be taught inwardly, as they were taught when the Holy Spirit descended on them. It was then that they received in answer to their humble request a sublime gift of prayer which was imparted to them by this divine Spirit.

Who prevents us from receiving the same gift in the degree to which it may please God to give it us? Can we doubt that Jesus Christ is willing to give it to us? But do we desire it? Do we ask it? Do we think we need it? How many Christians do not even know what it is. And how many others instead of desiring it are afraid of it, because it would commit them to a perfection to which they no longer aspire.

We know by heart a few forms of prayer; we find others to choose from in books; there we stop, and when we have read these or recited them by heart we imagine that nothing else is required. How grievously we deceive ourselves! With all these forms, however beautiful the sentiments expressed, we do not know how to pray and mostly we do not pray; or perhaps we are praying in our own way, but we are not praying in God's way. Where is the Christian who would not be shocked if he were accused of not knowing how to pray? Where is he whose chief prayer is to beseech God to teach him how to pray? Nevertheless the truth is that nearly all are very ignorant on this subject and that God alone can teach them by speaking to their hearts; the truth is, in fact, that it is only spiritual souls quickened by grace who rightly pray according to God's will, whatever be their prayer, vocal or mental.

To speak more precisely, I assert that God must teach us everything concerning the *nature* of prayer, its *object*, its *characteristics*, the *disposition* it requires and the *personal application* we must make of it according to our needs. That is to say that in the matter of prayer we are as ignorant of the theory as of the practice.

God grant that what I am going to say on this subject may be useful to my readers. I am sure that it will seem new to many of them.

We know in general that prayer is a religious act, but when it comes to praying we easily forget that it is a supernatural act which is therefore beyond our own strength and can only be worthily performed by the inspiration and help of grace. As St. Paul says: *Not that we are sufficient of ourselves to think anything as of ourselves, but our sufficiency is of God*[1].

Have we habitually this thought in our mind and in our heart the feeling of our own insufficiency? Are we conscious of it when we place ourselves in God's presence? Do we begin our prayers with this secret confession? I do not say that we must always expressly invoke God's help, but such an invocation ought to be in our hearts and such a disposition should govern the whole course of our prayer.

But if we are to look for everything from God, all our good thoughts and good feelings, how is it that some are so dull and indifferent, satisfied to say their prayers coldly without any preparation, as if it were enough to possess memory and eyesight? Why do others make such misplaced exertions, clasping their heads and exerting themselves and inflaming their imagination, as if all depended on their own efforts and it were not necessary that God's action should govern and direct their own? Since prayer is a supernatural act we must earnestly entreat God to produce it in us and then we must perform it tranquilly under his guidance; we must draw down divine grace by our favour and then we must co-operate with it without interfering with its effects.

If God does not teach us we shall never know thoroughly the *nature* of prayer and I dare to assert that many Christians, in other matters able and learned, do not understand it.

God is a Spirit, said Jesus Christ, *and they that worship him must worship him in spirit and in truth*.[2] Prayer then is in itself a wholly spiritual act, addressed to him who is the Supreme Spirit, the Spirit who sees all things and is present in all things

[1] 2 Cor. 3: 5.
[2] St. John 4: 24.

and is, as St. Augustine says, more closely united to our soul
than its deepest depths. If to this essential prayer we join a
particular attitude of the body and certain words and outward demonstrations, all this has no significance in itself and
is only pleasing to God as it expresses the feelings of the heart.
To speak properly, it is the heart that prays, it is to the voice of
the heart that God listens and it is the heart that he answers,
and when we speak of the heart we mean the most spiritual
part of us. It is indeed noteworthy that in the Scriptures
prayer is always ascribed to the heart; moreover, it is the
heart that God teaches and it is through the heart which has
learnt to pray that he then enlightens the mind.

If this be so, as we cannot doubt, why do we pray so much
with our lips and so little with our heart? Why do we not
draw our prayer from that source instead of resorting to our
memory and to our lips? Why in meditation do we work our
minds so hard in the search for considerations, and use our
wills so little to move them to acts of the affections? Why indeed do we not lay open our heart to God and beg him to put
into it whatever is most pleasing to him? Could you suppose
that it is a bad method which springs from humility, from a
deep sense of our own incapacity and from a lively faith and
trust in God, a method suggested by the Holy Spirit himself to
those souls who appeal to him to teach them how to pray?
"But my heart says nothing to me", you say, "when I am in
the presence of God; if I attempt to retire into myself I find
nothing but emptiness, dryness, distractions; if I am to fix my
mind, to arouse in myself some feelings of devotion, to drive
off distracting thoughts, it is absolutely essential for me to use
books." Your heart says nothing. In so far as it is silent, you
are not praying at all; and if it is dumb in itself, is it any less
so when your mouth is uttering words? Do you not see that
these fine feelings you borrow from books only affect your
imagination; that they are yours, or rather you fancy they are
yours, only for the moment that you are reading them, and

that once the book is closed, you are as dry and as cold as you were before? "At all events," you say, "I was praying whilst I was reciting or reading that set of words." So your self love thinks and is satisfied; but is that God's point of view? Is God equally satisfied? What do your words matter to him, to him who only listens to the heart?

You ask me what this voice of the heart is. How can I put it into words and how could you understand me? It is love which is the voice of the heart. Love God and you will be always speaking to him. The germ of love is the germ of prayer; the development and perfection of love are the development and perfection of prayer. If you do not understand that, you have never yet either loved or prayed. Ask God to open your heart and kindle in it a spark of his love; then you will begin to understand what praying means.

Is it then true that a sinner who prays to God from his heart is actually loving him? Yes, he has at any rate the beginnings of love, or how could he pray from the heart? It is that love which dictates the prayer to him. It may be that his love is not yet strong enough to justify him, but it is preparing him for justification and leading him on towards it. Can we say then that the just man who is inattentive, cold and unfeeling in his prayer, does not love God at all? If it is by his own fault that he is in this condition, he must still have the habit of love, since we are supposing him to be a just man; but he is failing to exercise love at the moment, he does not love actually, nor does he pray, since whilst his tongue is active his heart is idle. Holy souls, who are enduring the painful trial of dryness and whose love is all the purer because it is less sensible, do not be troubled! What I have just said does not apply to you.

If it is the heart that prays it is evident that sometimes, and even habitually, it can pray by itself without any help from words, spoken or conceived. Here is something which few people understand and which some even entirely deny. They insist that there must be definite and formal acts, at least interior ones, which are distinctly perceived and of which the soul must be conscious; apart from such acts they do not recognize any prayer. They are mistaken and God has not yet taught them how the heart prays. Now thought is formed in the mind before it is clothed in words. The proof of this is that we often search for the right word and reject one after another till we find one which expresses our thought accurately. We need words to make ourselves intelligible to other people; but they are useless for our own minds and if we were pure spirits, we should use no language, either to express or communicate our thoughts. It is the same with the feelings of the heart. The heart conceives feelings and adopts them without any need of resorting to words, unless it wishes to communicate them to others or to make them clear to itself.

But God reads the secrets of the heart; its most intimate feelings, even those which are neither formulated in the mind nor perceived by the soul, are open to him. And if these are religious and supernatural feelings how could he fail to see them, since it is he who implants them in us by his grace and helps our will to adopt them? It is not necessary to make use of formal acts, even such as are purely interior, to make ourselves heard by God; and if we do make use of them in prayer it is not so much for his sake as for our own, to keep our attention fixed in his presence. Our weakness often calls for the help of such acts; but they are not of the essence of prayer and God, when he pleases, from time to time raises the soul above all such needs.

Imagine then a soul so closely united to God that it has no need of outward acts to remain attentive to the inward prayer; in these moments of silence and peace, when it pays no heed to what is happening within itself, it prays and prays excellently, with a simple and direct prayer that God will understand perfectly but which it will not perceive itself, for it is as it were transported out of itself by the action of grace. The heart will be full of aspirations towards God without any clear expression; so spiritual that they will elude its own consciousness, though they will not escape the consciousness of God. This prayer so empty of all images and apperceptions, apparently so passive and yet so active, is, so far as the limitations of this life allow, pure adoration in spirit and in truth. It is adoration fully worthy of God, in which the soul is united to him as its ground, the created intelligence to the uncreated, without the intervention of imagination or reasoning, or of anything but a very simple attention of the mind and an equally simple application of the will. This is what is called the prayer of silence, or of quiet, or of simple regard, or of bare faith; a form of prayer where God gradually trains those who have truly given themselves to him, who are directed by grace in a special manner.

Souls who are favoured with this excellent gift will have no difficulty in understanding what I have said; they will recognize here the kind of prayer which holds them as it were prostrate in God's presence and wholly lost in him. Others will understand nothing of it; to use the Gospel phrase, it will be a word hidden from them. Let these however begin by respecting what they cannot understand, let them desire to experience this form of prayer and so learn its meaning, making it the object of their prayers and living in such a way as to deserve an answer from God.

If there is one favour more than another which God desires to give us it is this; but where are those Christians who are willing to prepare themselves to receive it by detachment and purity of heart? Where are those who having received the first-fruits are able to develop them by entire conformity to grace?

Those who cannot understand how the heart can pray alone without any distinct acts, cannot understand either how a simple general prayer can perfectly well include all particular prayers. It should be sufficiently understood without my mentioning it that I except prayers of obligation. In this matter people generally treat God as though he were a man, and believe that he cannot understand a prayer unless every detail of its requests is explained to him. They prepare carefully their intention, have special formulas for each act of prayer, mention individuals by name and imagine that if the least detail escapes their memory God cannot supply it. O souls of little faith and little knowledge of God, your intentions have reached him before you have opened your mouth; no sooner are they in your heart than he sees them, and why must you torment yourselves by explaining them to him? You desire every spiritual blessing both for yourselves and for those whom you love; how should he who inspired these desires not know that you have them? Have no anxiety then in this matter and if you feel any attraction for the simple and general prayer of which I have been speaking, do not reject it on the excuse that it has no definite aim and that you rise from your knees without having asked for anything. Let me say it again, you are mistaken; you have asked for everything both for yourself and for those whom you love, and far more effectually than if you had made detailed requests whose multiplicity would only have exhausted you and hindered the action of God, which aims at keeping you in a state of holy calm in his presence.

After this brief explanation, you must see that you have not until now understood what prayer really is. If you are beginning to have another idea of it, thank God for it, for it is he who is teaching your heart and what I am writing here for your instruction comes from him.

O my Saviour, how much I needed to be taught concerning prayer! Why did I not know that it was altogether supernatural and was formed by thy grace in hearts prepared for it? I thought that it was enough to know the prayers learnt in childhood, adding to them a few forms taken from books; I thought that if I recited or learnt those I was completely performing my first duty. How grievous was my mistake! I never dreamed that words were only the outward part of prayer; that it was the heart that prayed, that the mouth only expressed the heart's feelings and spoke in vain unless it were the heart's interpreter. Still less did I think that the heart could pray by itself and that in intercourse with thee all language except its own was useless. Language of the heart, language so expressive and touching in God's sight, language of the Blessed Spirits, language used by the saints upon earth, how have I failed to use this language in speaking to God!

O my divine Master, teach me this mute language which says so many things. Teach me to hold myself in inward and outward silence before thee, to adore thee in the depths of my being, to wait upon thee always and never ask anything of thee but the fulfilment of thy will. Teach me to let thee act in my soul, and form in it the simple general prayer that defines nothing and expresses everything, that states nothing and includes everything. If thou wilt grant me this grace how faithfully will I devote a fixed time every day to prayer! How gladly will I carry it out and what pains will I take to preserve so precious a gift! Alas, Lord, I do not know what I say; I speak as though I were capable of making a promise or of keeping it by myself, and as though my promises could lead thee to do me good. Consider rather thine own goodness and grant me this favour for the glory of thy Name. Add to it the grace to use it well and to deserve its preservation and increase. Amen.

CHAPTER II

GOD ALONE TEACHES US TO PRAY
(*continued*)

The Saviour's teaching is no less necessary for most Christians
with regard to the *object* of prayer. I am especially referring to
the interior teaching of grace which not only enlightens the
mind but stirs up the will to action.

Prayer like sacrifice has four objects: *adoration, thanksgiving, the pardoning of sins* and *the obtaining* of spiritual and
temporal blessings.

The two first objects directly concern God and are for that
reason undeniably the most important.

The two last concern our own interests, which are subordinate to those of God and which should only receive our
attention after them.

From this it follows that whenever we appear before God in
prayer our first intention must be to adore his supreme
Majesty, to prostrate ourselves before him and pay him the
tribute of glory which is his due; secondly, to acknowledge
the benefits, whether common or personal, natural or supernatural, which his generosity has bestowed upon us and to
thank him for them with the deepest affection of our hearts;
thirdly, to testify our sincere sorrow for having offended him
and to beg for his forgiveness; and fourthly, to lay before him
the needs of our soul and our body, and place our spiritual
and temporal affairs in his hands, in complete trust that whatever he ordains will be most profitable for us. I am not saying
that we must always have each of these intentions actually in
our minds; but they must be in our hearts where they must

hold their proper order, so that God and his interests should always be our principal object and our interests should come second.

So in the ancient Law the burnt offering was the highest form of sacrifice; there the victim was entirely consumed in honour of God, to signify the consecration of the whole human nature to his service, and neither priests nor people had any share in it. So in the new Law the sacrifice of Jesus Christ was offered on the cross and is daily offered on our altars, primarily to do honour to God and to acknowledge his absolute sovereignty over his creatures. Jesus Christ had other intentions too but that was his first intention and the others were in subordination to it.

Now the order which our Saviour kept in his intentions when he prayed to his Father and when he offered himself, must be the rule which we follow in our own prayers, a rule which must never be varied. This need not prevent us from making the immediate object of our prayers the forgiveness of our sins, or our own spiritual needs, or sometimes our temporal affairs, as long as these do not interfere with the other and higher intentions, and especially the glory of God which must be essentially the aim of all prayer.

But self-love, which influences our prayers even more than it does other matters, reverses the order established by the very nature of things by divine institution and by the example of Jesus Christ. It cannot endure that when we are calling upon God or serving him we should think of anything but ourselves, or have regard to anything but our own interests. It can only think of prayer as a petition, a request presented to God in order to gain a particular benefit from him; it loses sight of the main idea of homage and the tribute of love and gratitude.

What would a sovereign or a master think of a subject or a servant who never approached him except with the idea of begging a favour? What would a father, a husband, a friend (for God allows us to approach him as such) think of a son, a wife or a friend, who never ceased to worry him with selfish requests? Yet these are the aims which self-love suggests to us and the conduct it makes us follow towards God. We pray to him only from a selfish motive; the whole object of our adoration and our service is to get something from him. Supposing we had nothing to hope for from God and were not forced by our needs to appeal to him, we should evidently show him neither respect, love nor gratitude. It is true that we are his debtors, insolvent debtors too, and he wishes us to ask for the remission of our debts; we are his poor, forced to beg at his door each day for the food of our souls and bodies. But are we not much more than this and have we not other duties towards God who created us for his glory, redeemed us, adopted us as his children, and bestowed on us so many tokens of his love?

A son honoureth his father, he says by one of his prophets, *and a servant his master. If then I be your father, where is mine honour? and if I be a master, where is my fear? What is the reverent awe that I have a right to expect from you?*[1] You come to visit me in my temple, you prostrate yourself before me, you offer me long and fervent prayers; but what is your purpose? Is it to adore me, to praise me, to testify your love for me and thank me for my gifts? Are such the pure intentions that draw you to my altars? Do you come to pay me the tribute I demand, to consecrate to me your whole being, to dedicate yourselves to my will and sacrifice yourselves to my good pleasure? Do you come to hold converse with the best of Fathers, with the spouse of your soul, the friend of your heart? I am all this to you, and you would please me much more and would be so much dearer to me, if these were the motives that brought you into my presence.

If we look into our hearts we shall be ashamed of the mean and mercenary ideas which form the bond of our communica-

[1] Malachi 1: 6.

tion with God. Are we not amongst those who, like the Jews, have no other object in their prayers but temporal benefits, who pray earnestly for the fat of the land but do not ask for the dew of heaven? Let there be some public calamity and our churches are full; in prosperous times they are quite empty. Suppose our private affairs go badly or we have some vexatious lawsuit or we are exposed to some serious loss; then we become very devout, we resort to prayer, we commend ourselves to our priest and devout friends. When we are anxious about our life or the life of a husband or a beloved child we have masses said, we begin novenas, we invoke the saints. Our needs and circumstances awaken our religion, as if there were no need to pray to God except in times of sickness or sorrow. No sooner have things taken a turn for the better and the danger is over, than our devotion melts away. We may perhaps offer thanks to God for our deliverance, but after a short act of gratitude we forget him and think of nothing but our pleasures. Speaking generally we may say that the necessities and accidents of life are the main matter and motive of the prayers of the majority of Christians.

Are we to be blamed, they may complain, for thus coming to him in our temporal needs? I am far from saying any such thing, for it is God's own intention to draw us to him by these means and we can do nothing better than turn to him on these occasions. What I do blame is that he is not invoked at all except for these needs, as if there were not for the Christian any other good or any other evil than what belongs to the present life. What I do blame is that God is forgotten as soon as these needs are supplied, as soon as the evils are averted and the goods secured. Indeed it is too material and carnal to reduce piety to such objects and such occasions.

I place just one degree above these Jewish-minded Christians, those who in prayer are only concerned with their salvation and who really think less of gaining heaven than of avoiding hell. Here again it is self-love that prompts and directs their devotion. This is not indeed wicked but it is very imperfect. They know that they have sinned but they do not know if God has forgiven them, or even if they have done what is necessary to obtain their forgiveness. Hence arise fears and excessive anxieties; all their reflexions tend that way. They aim at nothing else in their devotions but to make satisfaction for their offences; they see in God only his offended justice, and because this frightens them they seek only to appease it. If they hear mass, they offer the holy sacrifice for the expiation of their sins; if they join some confraternity, it is in order to participate in the merits of the associates and in the indulgencies granted to it by the Sovereign Pontiffs; in the same way they say the rosary and certain prayers only in the hope of gaining indulgencies; they approach the Holy Table with the same end in view, selecting particular churches and special days; if they do good works or practise mortifications, it is all for the same purpose.

All this is good, no doubt, and I have no wish to disapprove of it. It is a holy and salutary thought that leads us to detest and expiate our last sins and to guard against them for the future, even if our only motive is our own eternal welfare. What I do thoroughly condemn is that our intentions should be centred in this, and that we never for a moment lose sight of ourselves in order to fix our mind on God alone. Penance is certainly necessary but the principal motives that should prompt it are: the goodness of God which we have outraged; the claims of his justice which we have denied, and which must be acknowledged in our penance; his holiness which we have offended, for which we must make reparation; his infinite Majesty against which we have revolted and to which we must offer our tribute of glory in absolute subjection; Jesus Christ whom we have crucified afresh, and whose sufferings we for our part have rendered useless: his graces which we have abused and the necessity of our contrition for this abuse. These are the motives which chiefly should excite our sorrow and repentance, improve our prayers and move us to good works. They must surely be more efficacious in achieving real contrition, in appeasing the divine anger and in obtaining the pardon of our sins, than the fear of losing our souls or the desire of salvation. At any rate, as long as you pray for yourself alone, your prayers will not be as perfect as God wishes them to be and charity alone can make them.

So then those prayers must be reckoned imperfect which are limited to requests for spiritual blessings, dwelling in our own gain, the merits we shall acquire and the high degree of glory and happiness we hope to attain. Self-love has often a larger share than we imagine in the desire to keep our conscience clear, to correct our faults and to make progress in virtue; however small the share may be it is always too large, for self-love has no place in holiness which demands its complete destruction.

This kind of prayer would be good and even excellent if you could moderate those personal considerations, if you would look less to self and only aspire to be holy in order to please God, because he wills it, and in the measure that he wills it, and in the way that he wills it. Then the will of God would be your first consideration and your own spiritual interests would be regarded as subordinate. At the same time your prayers would be purer and more likely to be granted, for God will not refuse a prayer made expressly on his own account. You would have too more liberty of spirit, nobler and more generous feelings, a readier response to the movements of grace, more interior peace. You would become less hurried and restless, less introspective and anxious about yourself, less complacent about the virtues you have acquired and more ready to deny yourself. For all the imperfections that stain the whiteness of holiness, the obstacles that hinder it, the difficulties that impede it, retarding and thwarting its upward flight, come only from thinking of holiness as it concerns yourself, and what you desire for yourself; you wish to make

it your own possession, instead of looking to God and his
glory first of all; for, as St. Paul says, *this is the will of God,
even your sanctification.*[1]

When we have dealt with these various classes of Christians what a tiny minority remains of those who make use of
prayer chiefly for the two ends of which God is the object.

One of these is to thank him for all his benefits, general and
particular, to praise his goodness and love to mankind; to
acknowledge that every good gift comes from him and so
must return to its source; to recall the many graces he has
bestowed upon us, in spite of our resistances and ingratitude,
the many sins he has forgiven, the many dangers from which
he has preserved us; and thus to run through the whole course
of our life, where we shall find ample matter for praise and
thanksgiving. Tender and grateful hearts, hearts full of a
sense of their own misery and weakness, hearts ever dwelling
on the remembrance of God's mercies, have here full occupation in time of prayer and inexhaustible matter for reflection.

The other object of prayer is to think of God in himself, to
adore his supreme majesty, to contemplate his infinite perfections, to praise him; to honour him who is alone great,
holy, almighty, the one eternal, unchangeable, self-sufficient
Being; to rejoice with him in his glory and happiness, to love
him purely for himself, to desire that the whole world should
know him, love him and obey him; to count ourselves happy
in contributing to his glory: to offer ourselves to him and to
devote ourselves to the fulfilment of his adorable purposes.
How pleasing is such a contemplation to God, whether it
presents distinct ideas to the mind or whether it exists in the
heart only in an obscure general and undefined manner; how
pleasing, I repeat, is such a contemplation to God. What
graces does it shower upon us when it is accompanied by deep
humility. Nothing approaches nearer to the state of the

[1] 1 Thess. 4: 3.

Blessed, whose eternal occupation is to cry, *Holy, Holy, Holy*, *is the God of heaven and earth;* to say without ceasing *Alleluia, praise the Lord*, and to say *Amen* to all that he wills.

What I say of God must be understood of Jesus Christ, of the unspeakable marvels manifested in the two natures of his person, the mysteries of his life and the divine constitution of his religion. Here we have matter of contemplation for all eternity, and all that we shall think of it and all that we shall say of it in heaven, will be infinitely less than the truth.

Here I will observe that almost all those who confine themselves to vocal prayer generally relate their prayers to themselves; that more spiritual Christians who practise meditation generally use it as a means to the amendment of life, so that their reflections and acts of affection and resolutions have no other aim than the correction of their faults and growth in virtue. It is the interior souls who are the only ones who make God the supreme object of their prayers, for they are entirely devoted to his glory, his love and his adorable will. This will not seem strange when we consider that it is God who prays in them, God who praises himself and glorifies himself through them, and that, rightly regarded, their prayer is a more or less perfect image of what he is doing perpetually in himself.

Let us consider, in conclusion, how much we still need to be taught by God in this matter and to go to the school of his grace, since in our prayers we refer everything to ourselves, whereas everything should be referred to God. O that we might once and for all understand the truth that is both evident and certain, that our interests are included in his, that in loving him we love ourselves, and that he concerns himself so much more with us as we forget ourselves and think only of him!

You may say: If I do not think of myself, of my spiritual needs, of my salvation, who will think of them for me? But do you of yourself think of these things, or is it not God who puts into your hearts these good thoughts and desires? Does he never put into your heart thoughts that directly concern himself? Why then do you not dwell in them instead of always returning to yourself? Is it God, or rather is it not your own self-love, that makes you leave him to think of yourself? The very thoughts and desires which concern yourself are only given to you by him, in order to draw you little by little to a state of perfection where you will think more of him than of yourself. *My daughter*, said Jesus Christ one day to St. Catherine of Sienna, *think of me and I will think of thee.* He would say the same to each one of us if our hearts were like that of the saint. And why are they not, or why at least do we not try to make them so? How much is contained in these few short words! What an admirable rule of perfection! What a source of praise! What sure provision for the needs of our souls, when Jesus Christ declares that he will look after them if we cast all our care upon him, and think of him alone?

Must I then, you say, put aside every other subject of prayer and meditation? No, but make it your aim to think more about God than yourself when you are praying, and when grace moves you in this direction do not resist it. Do not yourself fix upon objects of prayer that concern you, and without anticipating God's action (which you must never do) do not put any insurmountable obstacle in its way; rather follow it faithfully with the help of an enlightened director. What a strange thing it is that we reject the kind of prayer best calculated to glorify God and sanctify ourselves. Spiritual directors who do not practise it should feel very humble for this reason, but they should not condemn it, or discourage those under their direction whom God is calling to it. They would be more cautious if they thought of the wrong they were doing to those souls, and of the glory of which they were depriving God. Abuses there are, I know, and they should be avoided, but if a director has not enough confidence in himself to preserve prayerful souls from these dangers, he should pass them on to someone else.

O my God, how clearly I see that I have never yet prayed to thee as I ought! I have not understood the chief object of prayer. Only very rarely, or perhaps never, have I approached thy presence with no intention but to pay thee homage; it has always been myself or my needs of every kind, that I have laid at thy feet. I am deeply humbled by the imperfection of my prayers and ask thee to forgive me.

Ah Lord, purify and ennoble my intentions; raise them to thyself and never let me keep them fixed on myself. Pray thou thyself in me that so my prayer may be ever directed to thy glory. Should I in thy presence have thought of anything but thee? Is it not right that my nothingness should be lost in thy immensity, and that the sight of my sins and imperfections should excite me to praise and magnify thy infinite holiness? Be thou then master of my mind and heart when I am praying; employ them solely, or at least chiefly, in adoring and loving thee; and may the thoughts that enrapture thy saints in heaven be my constant occupation at thine altars. Amen.

CHAPTER III

GOD ALONE TEACHES US TO PRAY
(*continued*)

Since it is true, as St. Paul expressly declares, that it is not we ourselves who pray but *the Holy Spirit who prays in us*,[1] and that our prayer is good only in so far as he informs it, let us see what are the essential qualities of that prayer of which the Holy Spirit is the author and let us compare such a prayer with our own, so that we may see whether the latter derives from him or from ourselves. Here we have great need of instruction, here we have a new and cogent reason to say to God: Lord, teach us to pray, not in our own way but under the guidance of the Holy Spirit.

What other prayer could be inspired by the Holy Spirit than a prayer which is *attentive, humble, reverent, loving, entirely confident* and *persevering*. If our prayer has not these qualities the Spirit of God does not acknowledge it to be his and hence it neither deserves to be heard nor can it be granted. Let us say a word about each of these qualities.

That a prayer addressed to God, whether to pay him homage or to plead with him for our highest interests, must be attentive to the point of keeping all our powers concentrated on that one object, is an assertion that none will contradict and that raises no difficulty.

Nevertheless, how few there are who pray, or even make an attempt to pray, attentively. I do not speak of young people, whose restless senses and lively imaginations offer them some

---

[1] Rom. 8: 26.

excuse for they are hardly capable of sustained concentration. At this age it is much indeed that there should be the intention to be recollected, that from time to time their attention should be recalled, so that as often as sense or imagination wanders they return quietly to their prayer. It is altogether another matter at an age when we have mastery over ourselves, and can fix our attention as we wish on any subject. That then in our prayers we should be the victims of an extreme and almost continual wandering of the mind, that this should happen not once in a way but habitually, that we should not think seriously about such an irregularity, that we should make no effort to discipline our mind, that we should have no bad conscience about it: all this indeed is unpardonable and it is only too common.

I will not here enquire into the cause of all this. I am considering the thing in itself, and I maintain that it is a shocking abuse to pray in this way and the chief source of the other abuses which bring discredit and dishonour on the Christian church. I maintain that it is a grievous offence against God, which makes us in a sense more guilty than if we did not pray at all. I maintain further that such inattention, which is only too visible in our bearing, scandalizes our neighbour, hinders him from praying and often discourages him from visiting our churches, where it is less easy for him to be recollected than it is at home. All this needs no proof and if faith is not quite extinct in those who have to reproach themselves with this fault, nothing more is needed to awaken the most lively and well-founded sense of alarm.

You would not dare to put forward the excuse of children and say that you are not master of your senses. But you are not, you say, master of your imagination, and it has not the power to withdraw your mind from the affairs which are your habitual occupation and which obsess you during your prayer. So it is that you pretend to justify your wandering thoughts. Yet you do condemn the curious glances that you cast all about you and the unnecessary, sometimes most unsuitable, words you permit yourself to utter.

But let me ask you this: when you pray do you seriously wish to be attentive? Is it your first care to recollect yourself and think what you are going to do. If you do not begin by this, if, on entering the church, or even on your way to it, you do not prepare yourself for so holy an action, your excuses are vain and you are responsible for your distractions.

Your imagination runs away with you, you say? Yes, when you are in God's presence; but everywhere else you know well enough how to control it at need. If you are asking a favour or discussing some interesting subject or speaking with important people, you are entirely absorbed in what you are saying and hearing. Act in the same way when you are speaking with God; I do not ask any more. Is that expecting too much? Does God deserve less attention than men? And is what we have to say to him of less importance?

Some visible object catches your attention and keeps it fixed when you are speaking to men, you say. Then you can have no faith when you are speaking to God, for if you had a single spark of faith, would it not light up in his presence before the Holy Tabernacle where Jesus Christ personally dwells and especially during the awful Sacrifice. The celebration of so great a mystery and our august ceremonies are surely sufficient to make an impression on you and hold your attention.

Your business affairs keep coming into your mind and you cannot keep the thought of them away. But why? It is because they interest you more than the business of your salvation, for the mind of man is so constituted that it dwells most on what most affects him. So that if religion really held the first place in your heart, there would be no room for anything else when you were fulfilling your duties, and all thought of worldly business would be, as it were, suspended. If it should assail your heart you would certainly repel it, and it would distress you to be occupied with it against your will during the time consecrated to God. This would be sufficient to free you from blame, because attention springs from the heart and one is attentive when one has the will to be so. I mention this in passing, for the sake of those good souls who are disturbed and grieved on account of involuntary distractions, sometimes even bad thoughts and temptations, which come to them during prayer.

God has his own reasons for permitting them and this is not the place to explain all this. But there are two things which should reassure such persons: first, their habitual recollection, which means that they only rarely give way to such distractions; secondly, their sincere desire to be rid of them and their grief at finding themselves thus overcome.

Another characteristic of the prayer formed in us by the Holy Spirit is that it is humble and reverent.

The very idea of prayer involves that of reverence and humility. He who prays is a creature; it is God to whom he prays. What is God compared with the creature? What is the creature compared with God? . . . This thought alone ought to fill us with the deepest humility; how much greater will this humility be when we remember that we are sinners and that God is infinitely holy; that we are guilty and that the God whom we have offended is also our judge. With what reverential awe should we not draw near to him. Is it not rather to be feared that we shall carry this too far and lack courage to approach God at all?

If you do not feel this, if you do not approach God with a profound sense of your own nothingness; if you, while the pure and holy beings in heaven cover their faces with their wings in his presence, if you, a sinner, are not struck by a holy fear, you should mistrust your prayer. It will not be the fruit of grace but of habit or human respect or any other thing but religious principle. Tell me seriously how you pray. What is your attitude and what is your general air and bearing? Can there be seen anything of the respect and submission that you ought to be feeling? Would you behave so, I will not say before an earthly king, but before someone whose rank was superior to your own? How well we behave then! Eyes, face, the whole body, how they speak. By our whole bearing what honour we pay to our fellow creatures, especially if we are going to ask a favour, to express gratitude or to offer some excuse! Or again how differently we conduct ourselves on certain ceremonial occasions, designed to express the honour due to birth, position and office!

These are only externals, I know, and there is much pretence on such occasions, but why do we affect such attitudes? Why does the world condemn any failure there? Surely it is because the appearance is accepted as the expression of real sentiments. Since you do not assume even these outward signs of reverence towards God, is it not clear that neither your mind nor your heart is moved by reverence, and that you are not aware either who you are or to whom you are speaking? For what is prayer unless it is an act of homage, and how can that be an act of homage fit for God which a man would consider an incivility or an insult?

The third characteristic of prayer is that it is *loving*.

God desires to be loved as much as he is respected and the Holy Spirit, who is the eternal love of the Father and the Son, inspires no prayer that is not a prayer for love and a prayer which leads to love. It is love, or at least the desire to love, which must inspire the Christian to pray; love must be the final aim, if it is not the subject of his prayer, and the increase of love must be its fruit. Even when the fear of God's judgments is the determining motive of a sinner or a righteous man, his ultimate object must be the attainment of God's love. If love counts for nothing, either as motive or as aim, it cannot be a prayer inspired by the Holy Spirit.

This takes us back to what I said before: it is the heart that prays and therefore loves or aspires to love.

When a sinner prays for his conversion, is it not as if his prayer were asking God for grace to love him? If he is truly touched, will he not express a warmth of feeling which is the first stage of love? There will be ardour, soul, life in his prayer; if it was cold and indifferent, the Holy spirit would have no part in it. If it is a righteous man who is moved to pray, still more will his prayer be rooted in love, since it is nothing but charity in action. If his heart was cold and insensible, it would be a sign that grace was not working in him at that moment.

Righteous men and sinners, you must both measure by this rule the quality of your prayers and the Holy Spirit's action within you.

Nevertheless there is a kind of insensibility, which is a trial through which interior souls have to pass, and which causes an alarm which is groundless. They imagine that they lack love in their prayer, because they no longer experience that sweet sensation of love that once was so delightful. They are afraid of having given God cause to forsake them and forthwith they are plunged in misery. But their very fears and distress should provide matter for reassurance, if they were in a condition to hear reason.

The heart that does not love is not at all alarmed because it feels no sensation of love; the heart that is distressed at the absence of that feeling, the heart that deplores it, cannot be without love, although it contains an element of imperfection and self-seeking. To a soul that has made some progress love is not a matter of feeling, but rather the determination of the will to do everything and to suffer everything for God; the more this love is deprived of feeling the stronger and purer it is.

Confidence is the fourth characteristic of the prayer that is taught to us by the Holy Spirit.

When it is he who makes us pray, it is plain that he influences us to ask only such things as he has resolved to give us, and that the first thing he grants us is a firm confidence that we shall obtain our request. This is the confidence that he answers and therefore he inspires it as an essential condition. It is our part to respond to it and not let our confidence be weakened by any fear or any kind of reasoning.

We see in the Gospel that Jesus Christ's miracles were all performed in response to faith: *Do you believe that I can restore your sight? . . . If you can believe, all things are possible to him that believeth. . . . According to your faith be it done unto you. . . . Daughter, thy faith hath saved thee.* He hardly performed any miracle in his own country and could not do so because of the unbelief of the people. The faith that he sought was not just faith in his divine power, but rather the hope that he would grant what was asked. He himself put that confidence deep in their hearts; often it pleased him to put it to the test, and he would only yield when he found the confidence unshakeable. Then he could not refrain from expressing admiration: *O woman, great is thy faith . . . Verily I have not found so great faith in Israel.*

Mistrustful and poor-spirited souls, who are always afraid that God will not hear you! Either your prayers are the work of your own mind or, if the Spirit of God is their author, you are not exercising the confidence he inspires in you, and it is for that reason and for no other that they have no result. Listen to the Apostle James on this subject: *If any lack wisdom let him ask of God . . . and it shall be given him. But let him ask in faith, nothing wavering. For he that wavereth is like a wave of the sea driven with the wind and tossed. For let not that man think that he shall receive anything of the Lord.*[1] Attend carefully to the metaphor he uses. If the Spirit of God were the only wind that blew on you, he would incline and urge your heart in the same direction, that is to say the direction of confidence; but your mind is blowing at the same time from the opposite quarter and from this your doubts and waverings arise.

[1] Jas. 1: 5, 6, 7.

Lastly, the prayer produced by the Spirit is persevering. It is not easily rebuffed; it is indifferent to apparent refusals but returns to the charge until God yields to its constancy.

Remember the example of the woman of Canaan. For various reasons owing to his wisdom and kindness God wants us to wait a long time for the favours we ask of him. He wishes us to put a higher value on his graces that we may be more careful to preserve them, since they have cost so much to obtain. Sometimes he wishes to grant them in greater measure than we ask and for this reason obliges us to pray more fervently. Also he wishes to mortify a certain natural eagerness which spoils the simple purity of grace, and to give us a holy and calm indifference. He wishes, moreover, to save us from the presumption into which we might fall if our prayers were heard as soon as they were made; we are so vain that there would be a danger of our imagining that we owed to our merits what came only from his liberality.

So let us guard against impatience in our prayers. As a rule this means that we are strongly affected by pride; the least appearance of refusal piques us, we reckon that God should give us everything at once, whereas the delays should only make us conscious of our unworthiness. Let us equally beware of the discouragement that comes from laziness, cowardice and inconstancy. Let us be humble and patient and let us never doubt that, if our requests tend to the glory of God and our own salvation, they will be granted in the end. If our requests are not granted, it is because they will tend neither to his glory nor our own benefit; and so we should not wish to obtain them. God has promised to open the door to him who knocks, but he has not said that he would not keep him waiting. He has fixed the right time to give us the boon, and likewise the right time for us to be inspired with the first thought of seeking it. Whenever we have reason to believe that this thought is from him, we must persevere in our prayer, being certain that he will reward our perseverance.

It is not often that all these qualities are found together in the prayer of most Christians. The majority, even of really pious souls, pray rather by routine than otherwise. They make their choice of set forms, based rather on their own preference than on the guidance of the Holy Spirit; they recite these well enough, or at least well enough to satisfy themselves as long as the imagination supports them and the sentiments continue to make an impression on them. But when these formulæ have no longer the merit of novelty and habit has dulled the taste, they recite them mechanically without affection and without reverence, at any rate interior reverence, and without love or confidence. They then decide to substitute other forms, the first forms having been thrown away as useless.

It is only the truly devout souls who are *led by the Spirit of God*, to use St. Paul's phrase, who habitually frame prayers that are really adequate and such souls seldom have voluntary distractions. It is impossible to see them so still, recollected and absorbed in God, for whole hours together, without being edified and filled with a holy envy. God holds them fixed in profound reverence, and the impression made on their souls by the divine Majesty irradiates their faces. The ground of their prayer is love alone and, even when their own needs are its immediate object, the glory of God is always its end. Their confidence and perseverance never fail; they pray with the firmest faith, expecting everything of their heavenly Father's bounty and know that if he delays to grant their requests it will only be for their greater good. So they are never weary, never become impatient, never complain; the smallest natural impulse of this kind gives them a pang of reproach. I can represent only imperfectly the qualities of their prayer, which rises every day to greater heights as they advance in the spiritual life. Only experience can help us to understand it and these souls are so simple, so detached from self, so lost in God, that they do not allow their minds to dwell on their method of prayer, lest its simplicity should be marred.

Alas, Lord I have only too much need to dwell on my manner of prayer, that I may condemn it and reform it. I do not see in my prayers any of the essential qualities. Hardly ever do I pray with the attention that is necessary, and I bring to it a mind that is distracted and a heart that is cold. I show thee little reverence, outward or inward, and still less love. My trust is weak and wavering; I have a secret fear that thou wilt not grant my requests, so forgetting thy kindness as not to speak to thee as to the best of fathers. Thence springs my lack of patience and perseverances. I want to have immediately and all at once everything that I ask; I give up correcting my faults, practising the virtues, and beseeching thee to help me in all this, because I do not suddenly become as perfect as my self-love would wish. How can I become good when I pray so ill?

O my Saviour, teach me to pray then no more in my own way and according to human wisdom, but according to the method of the Holy Spirit. May he quicken me and pray in me with those "groanings which cannot be uttered" of which thine Apostle speaks. Amen.

CHAPTER IV

GOD ALONE TEACHES US TO PRAY
(*continued*)

We now know the nature, the objects and the qualities of prayer. We have next to discover the dispositions that it demands of us. This enquiry is not difficult and it is easy to infer them from what has been said above.

But in order to bring the matter home to us and make us determined to strive earnestly after the dispositions which may forward the Holy Spirit's prayer within us, I must begin by stating two principles.

The first is that salvation and the whole business of Christain perfection depends on prayer. For God in the ordinary course of his providence has made the graces which lead to perfection dependent on prayer. We shall therefore certainly obtain them if we pray well. Now since of all the graces the most precious is that of steadfast fidelity, and since it is also the one which the Christian who prays well is most earnest in asking, it will be granted to him along with the others. Thus he will receive the graces God has destined for him and he will make good use of them; therefore in praying well he will arrive at the degree of sanctity that God intends for him, and to the corresponding degree of glory and beatitude. The whole sequence forms a chain whose first link is prayer. That is quite certain. If anyone does not receive the graces he needs or if he makes a bad use of them it is because he has grown slack in the practice of prayer; the decline of the Christian life always begins at that point. In other respects a man may receive some slight wounds and have a few falls; but

44

if he does not give up his prayer, if he is always trying to acquit himself well, it mends all wounds, it renews and restores everything. Prayer is a preservative, a universal remedy.

The second principle is that the Christian's prayer is always good when the Holy Spirit prays in him, on the contrary it is more or less defective in proportion as the human element enters into it. I have already asserted that prayer is a supernatural action and must therefore be produced by a supernatural cause; so that the more fully this cause acts and the less it is thwarted by the obstacles man puts in its way, the more excellent is the prayer. This supernatural cause is none other than the Holy Spirit who, when he inspires our prayer raises us above our natural weakness and in proportion to our co-operation with him, prevents the admixture of any imperfection in our prayer. If our prayer is all his, with a simple co-operation on our part, it is altogether divine and although there is almost always some involuntary imperfection, this does not prevent the prayer from being fundamentally the Holy Spirit's prayer; it simply means that a man with the best will in the world prays more or less imperfectly according to his actual state at the moment.

It follows from these two principles that it is of the greatest importance to us that the Holy Spirit should be the director of our prayer, and that we must make every effort to bring that about.

But does it depend on us? Yes, it does. The Holy Spirit desires to pray in us; that is clear, for he wishes our prayers to be good prayers and without him they cannot be so. If he does not pray in us, either absolutely or with all the freedom he desires, the impediment comes and can only come from us. Think well about this; if you have hitherto given it no serious thought, think of it very seriously in the future. It depends entirely on you that your prayer should be the Holy Spirit's prayer and that in time it should be wholly his, in proportion as you permit him to take more and more control over your soul.

What must I do then to bring this about? you ask me. For I have the strongest desire to cease to pray in my own strength and I understand all the advantages of being guided by the Spirit in this matter, but I do not see how to accomplish it. The more vehemence I put in my prayer, the more effort I make, the more it will be myself who prays. If I make no effort and if I wait for the Holy Spirit to begin, I fall into idleness and become the pray of illusion. For the rest, as far as I can see, this prayer of the Holy Spirit is an advanced form of mental prayer; it is a gift of God which I cannot have by my own effort, and in the opinion of all masters of the spiritual life it would be a most dangerous error to wish to enter on my own initiative upon this way of prayer.

Here is the answer to your difficulty: it is not only mental prayer that the Holy Spirit creates in us, but also vocal prayer, meditation, aspirations, active contemplation. I agree however that mental prayer is the foundation of these prayers, when we are possessed by the Holy Spirit in making them. I do not suggest that you should launch out into such mental prayer if you do not feel called; it would be all to no purpose. The matter is not in your power with the ordinary measure of grace. As long as you feel drawn to vocal prayer and have the desire for meditation and the ability to practise it, do not give them up and do not try to advance by yourself to a more exalted state, but always begin your prayer and meditation by an invocation to the Holy Spirit which comes straight from the heart. Remember that, although you can utter prayers, with your mouth, you cannot pray unless he gives the first impulse to your soul. Remember too that your considerations and affections are not a prayer if he does not inform them, and pray that he would put your faculties in motion. That done, pray and meditate peacefully and without effort and remain always united in heart and mind to God, resisting whatever can distract your attention. This is all that you have to do and this too is all that the Holy Spirit requires of you, in order that your prayer and meditation may be his.

Observe one point, however, that is of the first importance. If, when you are meditating or reciting vocal prayers, you should feel a specially strong sense of God's presence, if you should feel a sweet sense of grace and be inwardly drawn to silence, that would be a sign that the Holy Spirit is taking possession of your soul in a special way and that he is giving you, as a first fleeting blessing, the gift of the higher mental prayer. In that case you should be silent and calm your faculties, resting quiet and passive under the operation of the Holy Spirit.

For when his action becomes sensible in this way it must not be disturbed in the least degree by any action of ours, but we must yield to it and assist it by a very simple acquiescence. If this action became longer and more frequent you would be justified, after consulting someone of experience in the interior life, in believing yourself called to the higher mental prayer and bound to follow that calling.

Would you like to know what can prepare you for this gift of mental prayer? Three things: humility, simplicity, docility.

Be continually humble in all that pertains to prayer. Be always willing to depend on the Holy Spirit for your prayer; do not rely on your own efforts to give you devotion but wait always on him. Believe that you are not worthy of his favours, do not desire them too intensely, do not envy those souls to whom he grants them. Rather you should be aware of your own nothingness, satisfied to remain there as in your rightful place without aspiring to any heights.

I would rather you spent all your life in the humble practice of vocal prayer than that you should have the least shadow of self-esteem, or feel yourself superior to others because of your wonderful prayers. Most souls that God has led on from the ordinary paths of prayer have not deserved that grace, have never thought about it and did not even know the nature of it; but they remained humble. Their first feeling was one of astonishment that God had deigned to regard them; God himself in calling them to this intimate communion with himself aimed chiefly at bringing their humility to perfection, and if they had not responded to his designs they would have sunk lower than they were before.

Be *simple* in your piety. Do not rely upon your intellect or upon the subtlety and depth of your reasonings. Real piety is not concerned with thoughts but with the affections. Do not use so many books and exercises and methods. Let your heart tell you what you wish to say to God and say it simply without bothering too much about the words; it is ridiculous to be eloquent in his presence and take a pride in prayers that are well composed, instead of using those that are more natural to you.

Simplicity is the characteristic of all real prayer and nothing pleases God better. He does not want so much formality in his service; great harm has been done by the reduction of devotion to a fine art dependent on so many rules. After all, everything depends on the Holy Spirit; it is he alone who teaches the true way of conversing with God and we see how, when he lays hold of a soul, the first thing he does is to withdraw it from all the rules made by men.

Much importance is attached to hearing Mass, making one's confession and communion in accordance with certain rules given in books. I shall always believe that it is a great mistake to become so attached to these observances as not to be able to do without them, for we may so come to rely on their help as not to think of drawing on the resources of the heart or of appealing to the Holy Spirit, although true prayer is formed by the co-operation of the two. I recommend the reader therefore to try gradually to pray without books, even though he may feel for a time some dryness or awkwardness; to ask Jesus Christ confidently for the thoughts and feelings he desires we should have during the Holy Sacrifice, and to appeal to the Holy Spirit for the disposition necessary for a good confession; and, above all, in communion to surrender himself entirely to Our Lord, relying on him for the best preparation and act of thanksgiving. Oh, how excellent it would be if we made nothing of ourselves, casting ourselves upon God that he might do everything in us! I am quite sure that we should find it more profitable and I have made the experiment more than once.

This was the practice of the first Christians who were far more advanced than we are in the way of devotion, and received the body of Christ with more fervour and spiritual profit. A great number of good simple souls, very easy to recognize, are quite ready for the higher degrees of prayer; they are only waiting for a director to introduce them and relieve them from the great number of their exercises, which they dare not give up without advice. But, to discover these souls, the director must be inspired by the Spirit of God and himself advanced in the path of mental prayer.

Lastly, be docile to the promptings of the Holy Spirit. To this end study carefully, but without too much curiosity, what happens in your heart and when you feel grace moving you, respond to it. The wind bloweth where it listeth; but when it blows the soul must not set up the least resistance; its duty is to let itself be carried where it is taken; habitual obedience to grace is the disposition that prepares the soul most surely for mental prayer.

That involves more than you would think. For we must not suppose that the Holy Spirit will come to us in prayer, if at other times of the day we do not attend to him or repel him and grieve him. We do not attend to him, we cannot even hear him, when we are distracted; and if a man is distracted at ordinary times, he will be distracted also at the time of prayer, whatever effort he makes against it. Good prayer demands recollectedness and recollectedness is in turn the fruit of good

D

prayer. We repel and grieve the Holy Spirit when we do not obey his admonitions, or do not heed his suggestions. At first he does not fail to reproach us at the time of prayer, but if this has no effect he withdraws and leaves us to pray alone.

It is our refusal of some particular demand that God makes on us which almost always closes the door to mental prayer for so many souls. For a long time they evade the matter, they promise and do not hold to the promise and in the end they become obstinate; then they deceive themselves into believing that they were not at fault and that the interior life was not for them. Self-love how cunning you are in deception! But you do not deceive the conscience. Whoever you are who read these lines, God may be speaking to your heart and saying: Yes, you did not wish to make that sacrifice to me, to overcome that fault, to give up that habit and this it is that has deprived you of so great a blessing; frankly recognize your fault, there is still time to put it right; satisfy God if you will satisfy yourself.

I do not know if there are many humble, simple and docile souls who, happening to meet at a certain time of life a competent director, have failed to arrive at mental prayer. But I do know that it is souls of this kind only that God blesses with such a gift, or that they at least are happy enough to keep it.

Observe that everything hangs together in the Christian life, and that if you take away one part the whole structure falls to the ground. You would like to be with the Holy Spirit during prayer and have the rest of your life to yourself; it is a delusion. Either the divine Spirit will govern all your actions, or he will cease to control your prayers. You would like him to possess you but only at intervals, to come to you and to leave you as you wish. That is not possible; he will not depend on you but he would have you depend on him. If he begins once to pray in you, his intention is to continue with-

out interruption and to hold your heart in a permanent state
of union with God; he will insist on a habitual recollection
and, if you continue to forsake this recollection, he will
punish you by forsaking you at the time of prayer; he will
demand from you a continual fidelity to all his inspirations
and if you forsake him, after having reproached you unsuc-
cessfully, he will end by leaving you at the times when you
are most anxious to keep him with you. In all this you have
no right to blame him. For what does he intend when he
would pray in you and what is it that you yourself ought to
intend? Is it only to spend a few delightful moments with
God? Certainly not; it is to obtain all the graces necessary to
consecrate all the actions of the day. But how will you consecrate them if the Spirit of God is not always present with
you influencing your heart, and if you do not keep yourself
recollected, attentive and docile to his suggestions? As soon as
your prayer is finished you withdraw yourself from his direction, throw off his guidance and return to your own way; so
now you are distracted, given over to thoughts useless or even
evil, a prey to your weakness, to the evil of your own nature,
exposed to the temptations of the world and to the snares of
the tempter.

Examine yourselves therefore in God's sight and see if your
disposition is humble, simple and docile, and if you sincerely
desire it to be so and are constantly striving to make it so. In
that case you have every reason to hope that God will favour
you with the gift of mental prayer.

Why then is this gift that God would gladly make common
so very rare? It is entirely our own fault. Instead of desiring it,
we fear it; instead of preparing ourselves for it, we deliberately
and often systematically do everything that is calculated to
keep it away. And why have we this fear? It is because we
always wish to be our own masters up to a certain point and
never to belong altogether to the Holy Spirit. His control
would take us too far and commit us too much; we have not

absolutely renounced sanctity, but we want to be holy in our own way and not in God's way.

Here I am putting a finger on the deep-rooted disposition of most of those who make a profession of piety. They carefully hide it from themselves because it is bad; but, in truth, it is this and this alone that hinders the operation of the Holy Spirit and prevents him from praying in us. Other reasons are given and so many excuses are made. They are just self-deception and deception of others. Nothing that God has implanted in us, no state of life, no profession or employment which is ordained by Providence, is an invulnerable obstacle to the bestowal and exercise of the gift of prayer. It is equally suitable for the young as for those of more advanced years, for the sick as for the healthy; everything that leaves us the free use of our reason leaves God free to use his grace, and it depends on us to use it when it is offered to us.

O my Saviour, I say to thee again with more insistence than ever: Teach me to pray; implant in me all the dispositions needful for the prayer of the Holy Spirit. Make me humble, simple and docile; may I do all that is in my power to become so. Of what use is my prayer if the Holy Spirit does not pray with me? And if my prayers are not good, what will my life be? If it is not actually wicked it will always be in danger of being so, and in any case always full of faults and subject to a host of little sins.

Come Holy Spirit, come to dwell and work within me! Take possession of my understanding and of my will; govern my actions not only at the moment of prayer but at every moment. I cannot glorify God nor sanctify myself save by thee.

CHAPTER V

GOD ALONE TEACHES US TO PRAY
(continued)

St. Paul, when writing to the Galatians, says to them: *Because ye are sons,*—distinguishing them from the Jews, who were slaves,—*God hath sent the spirit of his Son into your hearts, crying: Abba, Father.*[1]

The Christian, you see, is a child who prays to his Father. The Trinity in concert forms his prayer; the Father and the Son send their Spirit into his heart; and if prayer is especially attributed to the Holy Spirit it is because he is Love, and the prayer of a son to his father should be inspired by love.

The same Apostle writes to the Romans: *The Spirit also helpeth our infirmities* (in prayer), *for we know not what we should pray for as we ought; but the Spirit itself maketh intercession for us with groanings which cannot be uttered. And he that searcheth the hearts knoweth what is the mind of the Spirit, because he maketh intercession for the saints*—that is to say the Christians—*according to the will of God.*[2]

These two passages of the Apostle contain the foundation of the doctrine of prayer which I have explained, as it would be easy to show. But in order to pass to what still remains to be said, I would only stress these words: *We know not what to pray for as we ought;* and on these words: *The Spirit maketh intercession for the saints according to the will of God.* These words have a direct bearing on the application of prayer to our spiritual and temporal needs, which is the last topic I have

[1] Gal. 4: 6.
[2] Rom. 8: 26, 27.

53

to consider and on which the teaching of our Saviour is most necessary.

Indeed, since nearly all our prayers consist of petitions, it is of extreme importance that we should make such petitions to God as it would be both in his interest and in ours to grant. For he cannot grant what would injure his glory and our salvation, or even what would be merely useless, and a Christian is not allowed to wish such prayers to be granted.

Now the Apostle clearly asserts that we do not know what we ought to ask in the way of either temporal or spiritual gifts, whether for ourselves or for those we love. We know well enough in a general way that God's glory is increased by his being known, loved and served by his creatures; but what exactly is the order of his designs, and the means whereby he is to be glorified in the particular circumstances of times, places and individuals, all that remains his own secret. Similarly, we have a general idea of what serves or hinders our salvation, but we do not know the decrees of Providence in this respect, or what means and methods will be used, or whether a particular temporal or spiritual situation will be favourable or the reverse.

Our own prayers however nearly always revolve round particular objects, about whose relation to God's true interests and our own we have only a dim idea.

In temporal matters we pray to be delivered from some particular difficulty, some illness or infirmity; to be enabled to carry out some plan or succeed in some business affair, or we pray that a certain individual may live. But do these things magnify God's glory or tend to the good of our souls? As to all such questions we are entirely ignorant, and we do not give them enough thought when we pray. Do I know whether this would be for God's glory? Do I know whether that would be for my spiritual good or that of my neighbour? To ask such questions as these would often be to defer our prayers and to resolve to leave the whole matter in God's hands.

We consider everything in relation to the present moment, our sight extends no further, and so it often seems to us that the object of our prayers is good. But God who can see into the future foresees the results of our requests, and so his estimate is different from ours. For instance, it seems natural to a mother to desire that her child shall live and to pray earnestly to Heaven as soon as danger threatens. But God knows that the child will go to perdition if he lives, and ensures his eternal salvation by withdrawing him from this world. Or again, we pray for good health promising that we will make a good use of it, but God can see that we should abuse it and so offend him. We may pray for success in some great enterprise, or for victory in an important lawsuit which will secure our comfort, enable us to establish our children and give us the power to do much good; but God sees that if we became richer our wealth would lead us into sin, and bring about our condemnation.

Instances of this kind are infinite and we can never be assured of the good or bad effect of our prayers, if they were granted. Nevertheless we pray with a degree of anxiety, zeal and perseverance, which makes it quite clear that we are actuated by something other than God's glory and the good of our soul. For our prayers are less importunate, less urgent and less anxious, when they are concerned simply with these two objects.

I will not here say more about the impropriety and irreverence of assuming that God will favour our purely human passions and designs, as if he was to accommodate his Providence to our greed and our interests, instead of our duty being to consult his Providence, submitting our wills and desires to him in advance.

We are no less liable to be deceived in spiritual matters. Circumstances that we think are conducive to God's glory and useful to us in the highest sense, are often neither the one nor the other, and of this I could give you a thousand instances.

For example, you ask God to give back to you that confessor of which he has deprived you. It was for your own good that he did it, for he was hindering your spiritual progress whilst you did not suspect it, so skilfully did he flatter your self-love. It is God's will that you should go to another who will be less agreeable to your self-love, but who will help you to advance in solid virtue. You ask him to grant you certain graces which he has given to others, to give you the courage to practise the same austerities and to advance you to the same degree of prayer; but these same graces which have sanctified others would not suit you, and they have no place in the plan for your spiritual growth. God has called you to an ordinary life; extraordinary graces, these macerations and exalted prayers, would tempt you to pride and you would yield to the temptation. You pray that God would deliver you from certain temptations which torment you and keep you in constant danger of offending him; you think that you could serve him better if you were less distracted in that way. On the other hand God sees that these temptations are necessary to you to keep you humble, disposed to pray and ready to put your trust in him. His voice speaks to you as to St. Paul: *My grace is sufficient for thee; for my strength is made perfect in weakness.*[1]

You are a priest and you pray God to make use of your talent for his glory; you ask him to enable you to preach his word successfully, to write in the defence of religion, to work for the conversion of heathens and infidels. But God has destined you for obscure labours, the instruction of the poor, a ministry in a rural parish, the direction of a religious community, where you will glorify him according to his will and in a way less showy but for you safer.

Into how many mistakes of this kind do we fall owing to a piety that is ill directed, a zeal that is not according to knowledge. We wear ourselves out with desires and longings and

[1] 2 Cor. 12: 9.

prayers that are not in the divine order of things, and which would be harmful to us if they were fulfilled. It all comes from our ignorance of God's particular designs for us, the kind of holiness to which he calls us, the method of the working of grace, the inner depths of our own dispositions and our true spiritual needs. In the face of all this ignorance how can our prayers be anything else but misplaced, indiscreet, presumptuous and opposed to the aim that we ought to have in view.

What method then should we follow? Must we simply surrender into God's hands all our business and all our needs, and abstain from all prayers in such matters except general requests?

Strictly speaking, I believe that up to a certain point it would be better to keep to this general method. Masters of the spiritual life generally give this advice and it is followed on the whole by truly devout souls. Nevertheless, since it is certain sometimes that God moves us to pray for particular objects, we should be prepared to do so when we believe that his Spirit is prompting us. Here is the disposition at which we should arrive when we have no moral certainty of God's intention.

The first thing we must do in all our requests, is to submit our mind and heart sincerely to the promotion of God's glory and our own salvation, or the salvation of those for whom we are praying. These are two fixed points which we must never forget in any prayer. So our prayers must be conceived in this spirit whether outwardly expressed or only understood: *Lord, if my prayer is such as to bring the greatest glory to thee and the greatest profit to my soul, I pray thee to grant it.* Or, and this comes to the same thing: *Lord, in this request I have no other intention than to conform and submit myself to thy adorable will. I make it only on the supposition that it is pleasing to thee; otherwise have no regard to it and take all thought of it out of my mind.*

The second thing is to assume inwardly a state of equilibrium, so that one is indifferent to the success of the request, equally content that God should grant or refuse it. This must be so because, since we have no foreknowledge of his will which only the issue will make clear to us, we must not incline beforehand either to the one side or to the other.

The third thing is to refrain from showing such keen interest, so much ardour, so much eagerness in prayers of this nature. We have indeed every reason to doubt if it is the Holy Spirit who inspires our prayer, when our soul is not perfectly calm and resigned to all that God is pleased to ordain. It is necessary to remember that the soul's peace is never disturbed when its prayer is the Spirit's prayer; such a prayer however fervent is never unquiet. If there is any agitation, if it is too urgent and excited, it is an infallible sign that we are mingling something of ourselves in it, or even that it is altogether our own.

If we observe these three conditions, we may safely pray for every kind of temporal or spiritual need; we shall be in no danger of displeasing God, and whatever be the issue we shall always be in union with his supreme will. It is very rare that these three conditions are fulfilled in the prayer of Christians who are governed by their own minds; and all of us are thus self-governed more or less, except Christians of a truly interior life. As for these, the Holy Spirit, by whom they are possessed, lifts them above all personal considerations in the prayers they make for themselves or others; it is always God, his glory and good pleasure, that they put before them as their end. As regards the object of their prayer they have no will but God's will; they are in a state of holy indifference as to its fulfilment and, both during their prayer and afterwards, their soul is in perfect calm. Thus their prayers are almost always answered, because, as the Apostle says, *he that searcheth the hearts* sees in them only desires conceived and expressed by the Spirit *who maketh intercession for the saints according to the will of God.*

Not only are we ignorant of the things we ought to ask for, but we are also ignorant of the time and manner which will be most suitable for their bestowal.

Everything is governed with supreme wisdom by the will of God. The effect which he has ordained that a particular event, a certain grace, should produce in us, depends on a certain exact moment when he sees that our heart will be favourably disposed.

Earlier than that moment would be too soon; after it would be too late. What is useful to you to-day would have been of no use yesterday and will not be to-morrow.

In spite of this we commonly prescribe a particular time to God and become discouraged or annoyed if within that period our prayer is not granted. What pride! What blindness! *Who are you that tempt the Lord?* might be said to us in the words of Judith. *You have set a time for the mercy of the Lord, and you have appointed him a day, according to your pleasure.*[1]

Man's impatience is extreme, it suffers no delay; the more he is convinced that what he asks is good, the more he feels justified in requiring it to be granted speedily. Suppose, for example, that we are praying for the conversion of someone in whom we are interested, or whose return to God is very important to the Church or the State. Since our request is good in itself, we expect it to be granted instantly; our imagination takes fire, our desires are full of ardour, we assail God with great violence and are irritated by his delays. But God, who does indeed see with pleasure our good intentions, remains unmoved; we must understand that he has his own reasons for his delay, and must learn to await his time patiently. Often it is in order to give us something better than we ask or to benefit us in some way, that he makes us pray for so long.

For fifteen years Monica prayed with perseverance, ardour and confidence for the conversion of Augustine. She asked for one thing only, that he should receive baptism and abjure

[1] Judith 8: 11, 13 (Vulgate).

Manichaeism. But God designed to make him a saintly bishop and the most brilliant light of his church. If that holy widow had penetrated the secrets of God, she would have seen that he intended the sanctification of her dear son to be advanced by the absurd errors that led his great genius astray, and even by his bitter pain in tearing himself from the pleasures of the senses to which he was a slave. In his search for truth and in his treatment of profound questions, Augustine was all the more distrustful of his own intellect because it had led him so deplorably astray, and he was the redoubtable champion of grace just because he knew that it was grace that had done everything for him. I repeat that if Monica had understood the great designs of God for her son, she would have seen how adorable they were and would have prayed with even greater patience and submission. There can, nevertheless, be no doubt that her fervent and constant prayers which she was certainly inspired to offer, contributed infinitely to her sanctification.

Learn then to pray as it were blindly, never to appoint a time to God, never to cease praying, though he should make you wait as long as Monica; and to believe that if he defers his answer it is always for some better end.

Be careful not to let your imagination settle the manner in which the thing shall be arranged or to dictate to God, so to speak, the plan which he must follow. *Who are you*, I ask again, to presume to impose your views upon the Lord? Pray for the object itself when he inspires you to do so, and leave to him the manner of his answer without troubling yourself about it. Ever since impiety began to reign in France, God has raised up throughout the whole kingdom a host of devout souls, who have never ceased to pray to him with the utmost ardour now for this object, now for the other. Their prayers have been apparently useless, because they have urged God to do exactly as they desired; matters have gone from bad to worse; the more they redoubled their supplications, the more crushing were the blows that fell; Heaven has seemed to be in alliance with Hell; never was any plot hatched by human wickedness so completely successful; we have seen indeed religion and the monarchy brought to the last extremity. How many times have the faithful in their astonishment bitterly reproached God. If only he had not allowed the destruction of that order, if only he had removed a certain man from his post, or saved the life of a certain prince! Things would not then have come to such a pass. Sometimes I have seemed to hear Martha or Mary weeping and saying to the Saviour: *Lord, if thou hadst been here, our brother had not died.* They did not know that he had allowed him to die purposely, that he might bring him back after four days by the most wonderful of all his miracles. Those holy souls of whom I speak did not know either by what mighty blows of his right arm God would raise this kingdom out of the abyss, showing at the same time his justice and his mercy; they did not know that in order to act alone and glorify himself before these modern Pharaohs, he abstained from using the ordinary means by which his Providence works.

Let us make a practice then of laying aside our opinions and desires, whether we pray in times of public calamities in Church or State or whether we pray for our own needs, temporal or spiritual. But since the Spirit must dictate our prayers and God will not answer them otherwise, let us entreat this divine Spirit to pray in us for the public welfare or for our personal concerns, for ourselves or for others; to pray for all that he knows to be necessary or useful, and to pray not only for the things themselves, but that they may be supplied at the best time and in the best way. It is only in this way that we can glorify God, sanctify ourselves and bring everything to a success far beyond our desires.

Lord! after so many lessons, so full of truth and instruction, it will be my fault if for the future I do not pray well.

I see what I must do for that to happen. I must live the interior life, surrendering myself in all things and for ever to the guidance of thy grace. I must bring nothing to my prayer except thy Spirit; if my own should bear me company it will spoil everything. But will thy Spirit guide me constantly in my prayers if he is not my guide in all my other actions? That is impossible. I see better than ever that to learn to pray is to learn to sanctify oneself; and we can only become holy by the complete renunciation of our inclinations, so that we may follow the guidance and direction of the Holy Spirit.

I am then quite resolved; I will no longer be my own; I will submit myself to the dominion of grace. May grace alone teach me to pray, to live well and to die well! Amen.

CHAPTER VI

THE MULTIPLICITY OF VOCAL PRAYERS

When ye pray, says Jesus Christ, *use not vain repetitions as the heathen do: for they think that they shall be heard for their much speaking. Be not ye therefore like unto them: for your heavenly Father knoweth what things ye have need of before ye ask him.*[1]

It is a fault then to use so many words in prayer; and it must be a serious fault, since Jesus Christ takes so much care to warn us against it, and even compares those who pray thus with the heathen. Indeed he could not express himself more strongly. We should never have supposed that this was so had not the Gospel made this definite assertion.

The passage then contains some very interesting instruction for us, if we know how to interpret it.

The heathen idea of divinity was as low as it was false, for they degraded their gods almost to the level of humanity, believing them to have no knowledge of the needs of those who called upon them; and so they use long prayers to inform them. They imagined moreover that these gods, being subject like men to passions and prejudices, were not always disposed to bestow benefits upon them, and they exhausted all their eloquence to influence them and change their intentions.

Although Christians are very far from having such notions of the true God, whose knowledge is boundless and whose goodness is infinite, nevertheless in their ignorance and simplicity they come to deal with him as they might deal with a man. In making their requests they describe their situation at

[1] Matt. 6: 7, 8.

great length as though he did not know it; they explain their intention to him in great detail, apparently fearing that he might not understand it; they reproach themselves with having forgotten to mention a person or a circumstance as though God, who reads the heart, would not supplement their faulty memory; they expound all their reasons and enlarge on the motives most likely to touch him, as if the divine goodness itself was not a sufficiently strong motive; and they rise from their knees well satisfied with themselves after much speaking much insistence and many repetitions of the same things. Apparently, like the heathen they mistrust God, as though they could never inform him of their needs sufficiently, nor do enough to dispose him in their favour.

It is not faith, it is not even reason, that governs such prayers as these; it is the sense and the imagination. Again, it is uneducated people and especially women in general who are most inclined to err in this way.

Jesus Christ neglected nothing that could save his disciples from this fault or cure them of it; and he could not have made use of a more effective way than to tell them that by such prayers they would resemble the heathen. So he forbade them to use words in their prayers, since words are unnecessary for the answering of our prayers; God knows before a man opens his mouth what he has to say, and it is not words that he answers but the purity of the man's intentions and the dispositions of his heart.

When a child of the smallest intelligence asks something of his father, knowing that he is dearly loved by him, is he not content to express his wish and having done so to rely on his father's kindness? Does he think that he will obtain nothing unless he worries him and is constantly saying the same thing? It would be wrong of him to behave so and he would be rightly reproached for doing his father an injustice.

We who are Christians and God's children ought to treat our heavenly Father at least as well as we treat our earthly parents. A child hardly thinks at all of his own needs; his parents care for him and think of everything that concerns him. Are not God's care and tenderness as great as theirs? Is it right that having to do with such a Father we should be anxious about his care for us? Would not earthly fathers feel themselves wronged by such anxiety on their children's part? Why should not God feel himself equally wronged?

Do not suppose that because you must not use many words in praying your prayers ought therefore to be short. Nothing is further from the intention of Jesus Christ, who in another place bids us pray always without ceasing. It is vocal prayers that he wishes us not to multiply too much, especially those directed to a single object; but the prayer of the heart which is true prayer cannot be continued too long, and by it God is never wearied.

It we attend carefully to the warning our Saviour gives us here and draw the correct conclusions, we shall see in it an invitation to the prayer of silence. After stating our needs simply by word of mouth, if we choose that way, we are to keep silence and allow the heart to speak with its own peculiar eloquence.

Do not tell me that you can pray with your heart only when your are praying with your mouth, and that the moment your mouth is silent you become idle and inattentive. If that were so you would not be praying with your heart even while your lips prayed; you would only be following your words with your mind, and feeling would have no part in your prayer. The heart when it prays often invites and even forces the mouth to be silent; and if this silence is unknown to you the words of the prophet can be applied to you: *This people honoureth me with their lips but their heart is far from me.*[1]

The reason given by our Saviour to dissuade us from praying with a multitude of words is a clear incentive to the prayer of silence. *Your Father*, he says, *knoweth what things ye have*

[1] Isa. 29: 13; Matt. 15: 8.

E

need of before ye ask him. He does not therefore need your
words which tell him nothing. But elsewhere he lays it on you
as a duty to pray to him and to pray without ceasing. It is then
a silent prayer, a prayer which is wholly interior, that he expects from you continually, and he only accepts the other for
the sake of this.

How greatly you are to be pitied if you know nothing of
this interior prayer and never practise it.

It does not follow from the reason given by Jesus Christ that
we should never speak at all to God, because he knows beforehand the object of our prayer; it follows only that we ought
not to instruct him when we speak and that it is for other
reasons that he requires our prayers, whether vocal or mental.

Long vocal prayers seem to be the characteristic of those
whose devotion is only external. Jesus Christ reproaches the
Pharisees particularly on this account, accusing them of de-
ceiving widows by their show of piety and so obtaining money
from them.[1]

God forbid that I should impute such motives to those who
recite long prayers; but excepting such souls who pray thus
because they have never been taught otherwise, I think that a
good deal of self-love enters into such prayers, and that whenever there appears the slightest affectation it is natural to expect motives of conceit or self-love.

The objection must not be made that this kind of prayer is
authorized by the Saviour's own example; that in the Garden
of Olives in the long prayer that he repeated three times he did
nothing but repeat the same word: *O my Father, if it is possible, let this cup pass from me: nevertheless, not as I will, but as
thou wilt.*[2] We should be greatly mistaken if we thought that
the evangelist meant that Jesus Christ's prayer on this occasion was entirely vocal, and consisted only of the repetition
of the same words. His intention was to make us understand

[1] Matt. 23: 14.
[2] Matt. 26: 39.

what was the essence of this prayer which Jesus Christ uttered aloud, perhaps once only, perhaps not at all, but which was the deep cry of his heart throughout his cruel agony.

You disapprove then, you will say, of the rosary and the chaplet which consist only of the repetition of the same vocal prayers.

I do not indeed, but you must remember that the use of the rosary was introduced during a profoundly ignorant century, when the faithful for the most part knew nothing about mental prayer and could repeat no prayer of any kind except the *Pater* and *Ave*; and also that it was St. Dominic's intention that the recitation should be combined with meditation on the principal mysteries of religion. Those who say the chaplet have no intention of disobeying the injunction of Jesus Christ, or of multiplying *Paters* and *Aves* in order to obtain more surely an answer to their prayers; their intention is to devote a certain time to invoking God and doing honour to Mary by a method, approved by the Church, which is a very effectual way of kindling faith and piety in the soul.

The great advantage of vocal prayer, which to be effective must come from the heart, is to fix the attention of uneducated ignorant minds and the quick volatile imagination of persons who lack concentration, or are even attacked by temptation. Amongst such dispositions there are always some which are more or less voluntary, so that there must be an effort to correct them, and in this endeavour vocal prayer is a very efficacious help when it is sincerely offered from the heart. But, apart from such cases it is a good thing to relax the practice of vocal prayer gradually, and replace it by mental prayer, either in the form of meditation or the prayer of silence. It is impossible to give too much freedom to the action of the Holy Spirit on the heart; and that action which tends to draw us inwards, which brings with it peace, recollectedness and silence, cannot endure to be disturbed by external prayer which distracts the soul's attention.

Let me say a word about children.

Up to a certain age they are not capable of anything but vocal prayer. But when reason and especially feeling begin to develop in them, would it not be well to teach them that there is another kind of prayer which is more pleasing to God, and more useful to the soul? Could they not be led to it quite gently by being taught to begin their prayers by an act of interior adoration, to end them in the same way, and to make short pauses in the course of the recitation? This practice would be very profitable for girls especially, who can make use of their affections at an earlier age than boys and would be able, if well brought up, to give a quarter of an hour to mental prayer daily by the time they were ten years old at the latest. It would not be difficult to train boys in this habit at the time of their first communion and to persuade both boys and girls to keep it up. The Holy Spirit would make an unforgettable impression on these young hearts, and give them such happy moments as they would always remember. If later on they gave up the practice, this memory would recall it and in some moment of grace induce them to resume it. At any rate when a confessor spoke of it to them, or they read something about it, it would not be strange to them and they would understand it more easily.

The reason that people are so attached to vocal prayer and care for no other manner of prayer, is that in the first place they are attached too much to sensible things; in the second place, that they wish to be quite certain that they are praying, and think this certainty would be weaker if their prayer was altogether spiritual; in the third place, because they fear distractions and hope to reduce them by fixing their imagination and senses on a book. Some people for the same reason recite their prayers in a rather loud voice in order to hear themselves, without troubling to find out whether they are annoying or disturbing other people. How ridiculous they make themselves! We must endure such things in others; but let us at least be glad of the warning for ourselves and strive to be free of such faults.

My intention is not by any means to disturb and alarm Christian souls with regard to their manner of praying. I only wish to convince them that there is a more excellent way than praying aloud, viz. to beg the Holy Spirit to teach us; to try again and again to keep silence in God's presence for a few moments; to refuse to be discouraged if we should not be as successful all at once as we wish; to keep our imagination from taking fright at a method of prayer which seems altogether strange; to accustom our minds to it little by little. I can answer for it that those who follow this road with discretion will find it profitable, and will be glad that they made the effort to abandon their former practices.

I am not suggesting however that they should give up vocal prayer altogether, still less that they should despise it as being suitable only for the inferior type of soul. There would be intolerable pride in the notion that they could do without it, and they would infallibly be led into the delusion of a false spirituality. The most interior souls, those who are furthest advanced in prayer, still have their regular times of vocal prayer in the morning, the evening and during the course of the day, to say nothing of the prayer of obligation and public worship. The Holy Spirit, however strong his influence, hardly ever opposes any obstacle to these kinds of prayer but allows them entire freedom; or if he suggests their suspension it is only for a few moments. So I do not think that on any pretext whatsoever, except in some very rare and extraordinary cases, a Christian should pass a single day without offering or reciting some sort of vocal prayer.

Why then, you will ask me, does the Church use only vocal prayer? The answer is simple. It is because the liturgy of the Church is a public office, and even the priests who recite the breviary in private, do so in the name and for the sake of the Church; and because the sacrifice of our altars is offered by the minister in common with the faithful who are present, and who are supposed to join in the prayer of the celebrant and answer *Amen*, as is still done at sung masses; and lastly, because all the sacraments are administered by a formula laid down by the canons and no minister is allowed to make any change in it. Vocal prayer is public prayer; mental prayer is private and personal.

Lord! I acknowledge that hitherto, either for my own satisfaction, or from habit or from caution, I have practised only vocal prayer and I have neglected the simple prayer of the heart, which is less flattering to our self-love, which detaches us from the things of sense and makes us more spiritual. I am resolved to give my attention to it now and to devote a certain time to it every day. Bless this resolution and grant that I may be faithful to it. I place myself under the direction of thy Spirit in this matter and will have no other master but him and those through whose agency he teaches me. And in all my requests I will learn to speak little; to tell thee my needs simply, that I may thereby humble myself and turn to thee as the author of all good; and then to hold my peace and await the result of my prayers confidently. Give me simplicity, give me faith, give me love; then whatever may be the method of my prayer it will always be pleasing to thee and to me always useful. Amen.

CHAPTER VII

THE EFFICACY OF PRAYER

If there is one single thing on which our Lord insisted frequently and with the utmost force and lucidity, it is the efficacy of prayer. In one place he said: *All things whatsoever ye shall ask in prayer, believing, ye shall receive;*[1] and in another: *Verily, verily, I say unto you, Whatsoever ye shall ask the Father in my name, he will give it you;*[2] and again: *Ask and it shall be given you; seek and ye shall find; knock and it shall be opened unto you.*[3] Again, in order to encourage the confidence of his disciples, after saying that a father does not give his child a scorpion when he asks for an egg, nor a stone instead of bread, he added: *If ye then, being evil, know how to give good gifts unto your children, how much more shall your Father which is in heaven give good gifts to them that ask him?*[4]

I confine myself to these passages. There are many others that are no less definite; but these will suffice.

Let us here observe how far-reaching are the sayings. Jesus Christ makes no exceptions at all, whether with regard to persons or things or times or places. He confirms his promise by an oath, swearing by the truth i.e. himself. After this who can doubt the efficacy of prayer? Does it not seem clear that we have only to ask, since God has so clearly pledged himself to refuse nothing?

How then does it happen so often that our prayers are not heard? God's promises are quite definite; they cannot possibly fail and it would be manifestly blasphemous to think that he is

[1] Matt. 21: 22. [2] John 16: 23. [3] Matt. 7: 7. [4] Matt. 7: 11.

71

unable or unwilling to keep them. It is therefore clear that the blame rests entirely with ourselves.

In fact, to put it in a word, it is we ourselves who do not fulfil the conditions on which God has pledged himself. When he states so definitely that he will grant what we ask, he is assuming that we shall ask *what we ought* and ask it as *we ought* and, finally, ask it with *such motives and aims* as are suited to his action. Otherwise our prayer, though offered by a Christian, is not a Christian prayer; and if it is not a Christain prayer God is not pledged to grant it, nor indeed is it possible that he should do so.

Therefore, whenever we propose to ask something of God, the first thing we must do is to enquire of ourselves whether we ought to make the request, whether our reasons are good and whether God may be justly expected to listen to us.

But it is obvious that in making this enquiry we must not consider the matter from a human point of view, but that we must have regard to God's ideas which are very different from ours. In such an important undertaking it is not for God to conform to our views but for us to conform to his. How many petitions would remain unuttered if we always consulted God in this way about our requests! I cannot live without certain necessary things; therefore when I have not these and am unable to earn them by my work I am permitted to ask God for them, and to count on his fatherly Providence to give them to me by means of charity or otherwise. But there is no reason for me to be rich, no reason why I should not suffer a loss of temporal goods which, while reducing my luxuries and depriving me of certain comforts, will still leave me a decent livelihood. There is no need that my business enterprises should succeed to the extent of my insatiable desires; no need for me to raise myself to a state of life higher than that in which I was born; nor for me or my children to make a marriage from mercenary motives; nor for me to secure the distinguished post which flatters my ambition but which perhaps

THE EFFICACY OF PRAYER 73

I am not qualified to fill; nor for me to win some lawsuit in which my claims are perhaps doubtful. And so on—the number of instances is inexhaustible.

When therefore I make requests to God regarding such matters, either for myself or for those in whom I am interested, I am not asking the right things. These are nothing but heathen prayers, prompted by avarice or ambition, and I have no right to expect that God will answer them in virtue of his promises.

I meet with difficulties, disappointments, humiliations, troubles, temptations and crosses of every kind; if I pray to God to come to my help and give me strength to bear them, I am asking as I ought and am therefore entitled to hope that he will grant my prayer. But if I am praying to be delivered from my temporal and spiritual troubles because I dislike enduring them; if in my impatience I pray to be relieved of my life, it is plain that my prayer is not a Christian one but is opposed to the designs of Providence for me, and to the Gospel which bids me bear my own cross daily if I wish to follow in the footsteps of Jesus Christ. I should not then be asking what I ought and should be strangely mistaken if I thought that God ought to listen to me.

But, you will say, it is on account of the faults I am daily tempted to commit and the fear of falling that I pray for an end to these crosses and temptations. Ought not God to grant my prayer? No, he offers you with his grace the certain means of avoiding these faults and resisting temptation; let that be sufficient for you and do not go on asking God to deliver you from the things that serve to humble you and mortify you.

When a man intends to make a request to an earthly ruler, he considers beforehand with the greatest care whether the matter is worthy of that personage's attention and of such a nature as to gain his favour, and whether there may not be good reasons against it. The Majesty of God, his holiness, his very kindness, demand that we should take equal precautions in our dealings with him, so that we should not lightly and without discrimination lay all kinds of petitions before him. We behave as if our own interests, caprices and passions were all we had to consider in making our requests, and God must fall in with all our desires however unreasonable they may be. We are far too much like the mother of Zebedee's children and we deserve, no less and even more than she, that Jesus Christ should answer: Ye know not what ye ask; you would have ceased to ask if you had paused to think for a moment, and you would have understood that these things were not such as should be asked of God.

Not only do we ask what we ought not to ask but we ask in the wrong way, and the one is usually the consequence of the other.

To ask in the right way it is necessary that the Holy Spirit should ask for us with unutterable groanings. And who are the Christians whose prayers are inspired, dictated and prompted by the Holy Spirit? Are there many? To pray in a state of grace is not enough here; it must actually be grace that causes us to pray, our contribution being no more than simple co-operation. But have most of us any experience of the unutterable groanings produced in the heart by the Holy Spirit, we who are so cold, languid and inattentive? If our temporal or even our spiritual interests cause us sometimes to pray ardently, is this not due to a heated imagination, or to natural desires, or at all events desires that spring from self-love? The groanings of the Holy Spirit are as calm as they are deep, whilst our own are anxious and disturbed and do not arise from the depths of the heart. The groanings of the Holy Spirit arise spontaneously and we feel that they are not under our control; but ours are produced to order or aroused by an effort. The groanings of the Holy Spirit are ardent but submissive; ours express nothing but our own self-will and we are annoyed if they meet with no response. After expressing our desires we do not end like Jesus Christ with the words:

nevertheless not as I will, but as thou wilt. He who searches our hearts knows the nature of our groanings and can distinguish their sources, and if it is not the Spirit who produces them he is unmoved.

Our Saviour promises that whatsoever we ask with faith shall be granted to us; and our faith fails us, and we carry to our prayer the doubts and hesitations that are the result of our timid thoughts and hesitating precautions. It is true that we do not doubt the infinite power of God, but we do him no less wrong by doubting his good will. The confidence that springs from the Holy Spirit is so strong that it rules out all hesitation, so patient that it never despairs, so courageous that it only grows bolder in the face of difficulties, and becomes more hopeful when all appearances are against it. Dare we say, with our hand on our heart, that our prayers are inspired by a faith as lively as this? Why are we so easily discouraged unless it is from lack of faith? Why, when God keeps us waiting a little, do we reproach him for being deaf to our prayers? Why are we cast down, dismayed and desperate, when the storm instead of passing seems to increase and the dangers to become greater? What is the use of a faith that cannot endure the smallest test and is upset by the first obstacle? Are we surprised that our prayers are not heard? Considering the weakness of our faith it would be far more surprising if they were.

Lastly we do not pray with the aims and motives by which God is likely to be moved.

We hide from ourselves as best we can the meanness of our intentions and motives, but it does not escape the infinitely penetrating eye of God; far from accepting prayers that are soiled in this way he rejects and condemns them. Any motive that is not, at any rate, in the deepest sense, concerned with his glory and our salvation does not move him in the least. But how few prayers are pure, with no object but God's glory. How few souls there are who appeal to his dearest interests and pray to him for his own sake only! What could he refuse when it was evident that his glory only was concerned, and when the prayer indeed had no other intention? So noble an intention implies complete abnegation, entire death to self, the deepest love and the loftiest aspiration, and unhappily is very rare even amongst the most fervent Christians. St. Paul bids us do every single thing for God's glory, and how much more then our noblest action which is prayer. If we approach God with this motive, which is his own in all that he does, we shall never have reason to complain that he does not listen to us. We have the definite promise of Jesus Christ that whatever we ask our heavenly Father in his name he will give us. But, as St. Augustine points out, a request that is contrary to the order of salvation cannot be made in the name of the Author of salvation. I should add that, where salvation is concerned, it is the glory of God and his holy will that must be our first consideration. Where these two motives agree in inspiring our prayers they are truly offered in the name of Jesus Christ, and never can we call upon that adorable name in vain.

Are all our prayers concerned with salvation and do we chiefly desire even salvation with the object of glorifying God? Many ask for it, but only from the fear of perdition and a desire to escape hell; or else because they wish to be happy and have no more to endure. I do not censure these prayers; but, if the Holy Spirit was their main inspiration, would he also inspire the mean fears and self-seeking desires that make them imperfect? There are so many urgent prayers where the object is the correction of faults, the acquisition of virtues and certain graces, into which there enters always an element of self-seeking. I say nothing of prayers which are contrary to salvation or endanger it. We should rather thank God than complain, when he does not grant such as these. For the rest, good in themselves but faulty in their motives, we ought not to wonder that he often delays to answer them, until they are made with purer motives and less self-love.

Let us now imagine a Christian who in his prayers places

God's glory and his own salvation before everything else; who cares nothing for anything else, and is resolved to accept without question whatever contributes most to these two objects; who prays by the Holy Spirit and prays with unshakable faith; I declare that the faith of this Christian cannot be rejected, though he should ask for a miracle. It must be so because his prayer fulfils all the conditions that God demands, and having pledged his word God cannot fail himself. Then it is not the man who prays, but God who prays to himself for himself and who, desiring to grant a certain blessing, urges the man to ask for it.

So do not let us blame God any more but blame ourselves for the failure of our prayers. *Ye ask*, says St. James, *and receive not, because ye ask amiss.*[1] You are, moreover, arrogant enough to think that you ask well and unjust enough to throw the blame on God. Let us begin by learning to pray, which most of us do not know how to do; and when we have learnt, when we can ask what we ought and as we ought, then our thanksgivings will follow our prayers.

But, you will say, one can never be sure of having fulfilled all the conditions of true prayer. This is true enough; and what would become of humility if we could always be certain of praying rightly? What would become of simplicity if we were to be casting an eye on our prayers in order to pass judgment on them? What Christian would be rash enough to say to God: Thou wilt certainly grant my prayer because I pray well? It is this uncertainty with regard to the merit of your prayer which makes all complaint impossible and forces you to blame nobody but yourself. In all circumstances God will be always right and we shall be always blameworthy. Our pride would wish it otherwise; it strives to justify us in everything even at God's expense and at the expense of his goodness and the sureness of his promises and in this it is most abominable.

[1] James 4: 3

O my Saviour, since prayer is my greatest and only re-source, let me never make it useless, or perhaps disastrous, to me.

Do not ever answer my prayers unless thy glory and my salvation are the chief objects and aims of my requests. Do not ever answer me, if through ignorance, self-love or some human motive, I should ask thee for something which might displease thee or injure my soul. Have pity on my wretched-ness and weakness, for nowhere do they appear more plainly than in my prayers; our human nature always shows itself there. Ah! divine Spirit, when will they come altogether from thee? When will grace alone pray in me and pray that nature may be entirely destroyed in me, with all its malice and wicked-ness.

May prayer, the source of God's glory, the channel of every grace, the seed of all the virtues, the ground of all merits, the sole consolation of man in this vale of tears, be henceforth the most precious occupation of my life. How many hours have I lost which I might have spent so usefully and delightfully in prayer. How many prayers too have I lost by praying ill. If I have profited so little by my prayers it is my own fault; I con-fess it, I repent of it, and I beseech thee, O my God, to assist me in redeeming this great loss. Amen.

CHAPTER VIII

CONTINUAL PRAYER

This section on continual prayer requires, both for its own sake and for the consequences which flow from it, to be treated with great care and read with attention.

Men ought always to pray, says the Gospel, *and not to faint.*[1]

Let us weigh these words. *We ought:* it is a precept and not a counsel; it concerns a matter of obligation and not a counsel of perfection. If we fail in this we are sinning more or less seriously. *We ought:* it is a general duty which concerns all Christians. It is not said only for the ministers of the Church, not only for those who are consecrated by religious vows, but for all those who profess to believe in the Gospel and to follow it as their rule of conduct, whether they live in the world or are withdrawn from it. *Men ought always to pray:* not only to have a fixed time for prayer and not to allow a day to pass without prayer, but to make prayer our continual practice, never suspended or interrupted.

That these words: *to pray always*, must be thus understood is shown by what follows: *and never to faint*. The Gospel commands us first to pray unceasingly and then forbids us to cease doing so, thus uniting these two ways of expressing one precept. You will not find in all the Scriptures a precept which is laid down in stronger or more definite terms.

But this precept, if we understand it as applying to vocal prayer, or even to that form of mental prayer which we call meditation, is plainly impossible. So those who do not recognize any other kind of prayer, have thought themselves

[1] Luke 18: 1.

justified in restricting the obligation to certain fixed times. No doubt they would be right were there no other way of praying to God, except by the lips or by the application and concentration of the mind.

But the words of the Gospel take us further and might have opened their eyes to the necessity of allowing another kind of prayer, of such a nature that every Christian can practise it unceasingly.

What kind of prayer is this? It is the essence of prayer, the only kind that attracts God's attention and which gives value to all the other kinds, in a word the prayer of the heart. This prayer can continue without any interruption, as no other can. It is therefore evident that that is what is meant by the precept, and that there is no need to adopt a restriction which the terms do not allow. It is the prayer of the heart for their ignorance of which Jesus Christ reproached the Jews, the prayer pronounced by God through his prophet to be the privilege of the new order: *In that day*, he said, *I will pour upon the house of David and upon the inhabitants of Jerusalem the spirit of grace and of supplications;*[1] a spirit of grace which will prompt them to pray without ceasing, and a spirit of prayer which will unceasingly attract new graces to them; a double spirit which will maintain a perpetual intercourse between the heavenly Father and his children. It is this prayer of the heart of which the Apostle was thinking, when he bade the faithful to *pray without ceasing*,[2] and assured them that he himself made a remembrance of them in his prayers without ceasing.

But, I may be asked, how can the prayer of the heart be continual? I, on the other hand, would ask how it can fail to be so. We have agreed that it is the Holy Spirit who creates the prayer of the heart, whether he is actually dwelling in us or preparing to do so. Now, when once the Holy Spirit has begun to pray in a heart, it is his intention to pray in it always

---

[1] Zech. 12: 10.
[2] 1 Thess. 5: 17.

and it is our own fault if this intention is not fulfilled; for it depends on us to make its fulfilment possible by responding to his inward action, and giving him the entire mastery over our will; just as, when he wishes to take possession of us, it is our resistance only that prevents him from doing so and, when once he is admitted to our heart, he will remain there always if we do not chase him away. But the Holy Spirit dwelling in a heart would never be idle, if he had full liberty of action. And what should he do except the work appropriate to the Spirit of grace and of prayer, the Spirit of sanctification? He would keep the heart in a continual state of adoration, thanksgiving, penitence for sin, and prayer for the divine assistance for the avoidance of sin. This does not mean that definite acts of prayer would be made every moment; that would not be possible. But the heart would always be at the disposition of the Holy Spirit, to make such acts as often as he should please, and the germ of them would be preserved in the ground of the soul, ready to be developed as the occasion arose. This persistent habit is what I mean by continual prayer, and no one can deny that it might be and ought to be the habit of every Christian.

What then is this prayer of the heart? It is the immediate effect of divine grace. Actual prayer is charity in practice; habitual prayer is the disposition prepared for the practice.

It is as easy and natural to the heart to pray always as to love always. A man can love God always, without always thinking of him and telling him of his love. It is enough if he is determined not only to do nothing contrary to the love of God at any time, but also to take every opportunity of proving his love and to make acts of love, whenever grace prompts him to do so. Surely it is in this way that a mother loves her children, a wife her husband, and friend loves friend. The person whom one loves never comes into the mind without awakening a feeling of affection; one would gladly keep the beloved image always present, and if the mind is devoted to other objects the heart never is. It is the same with prayer. We are said to pray always when we should wish to do so if it were possible, when we never lose any opportunity of praying, and are constantly prepared to co-operate with the promptings of grace.

It would be to misunderstand the whole matter if we supposed that the occupations of life are a hindrance to this sort of prayer. On the contrary they are, or at least often may be, our way of practising it and there is a kind of prayer which is rightly named the prayer of action. Every action performed in the sight of God because it is the will of God, and in the manner that God wills, is a prayer and indeed a better prayer than could be made in words at such times. Nor is it necessary that the action should be good and holy in itself; it may be quite indifferent and yet none the less a prayer, in virtue of the intention with which it is performed. Thus the Apostle was once more exhorting the faithful to pray always when he said: *Whatsoever ye do in word or deed, do all in the name of the Lord Jesus, giving thanks to God and the Father by him;*[1] and again: *Whether therefore ye eat or drink, or whatsoever ye do, do all to the glory of God.*[2] If an animal action such as eating or drinking does not interrupt the continuity of prayer, it is still less likely to be interrupted by the labours of body or mind or of any kind of domestic affairs or by the duties of our occupations. There is nothing in any of these concerns in themselves to distract the heart from its union with God, nothing to arrest the actions of the Holy Spirit on the soul's inward conformity with it. That is an understatement; indeed all these things tend to unite us more closely to God and to maintain the hidden communion of the Holy Spirit and the soul. We are always praying when we are doing our duty and turning it into work for God.

Among the actions that may be regarded as prayer I would

[1] Col. 3: 17.
[2] 1 Cor. 10: 31.

include visits of politeness and good manners, provided they
are innocent and necessary relaxations of body and mind,
provided they are innocent and carried no further than is
allowed by Christ's principles; with the exception of things
that are wrong, inexpedient or useless, there is nothing that
the Holy Spirit cannot make his own, nothing that he cannot
contrive to sanctify and bring into the realm of prayer. Were
not the Agapes of the first Christians, which were instituted
by the Apostles, undoubtedly holy and seasoned with Christian joy? Did they weaken the spirit of grace and of prayer in
those who were present, or were they not rather a proof of its
power? Why should it not be the same with our meals, if only
we were like the faithful of those days? It is just this that I
find so admirable in the religion that we profess, that it teaches
us to honour God in everything, to pray to him at all times
and to practise virtue in all occupations, so that nothing is
allowed to be indifferent or useless in the life of a Christian.

But if there is a prayer of action, there is also a prayer of
suffering, and it is this which is the best of all and most pleasing to God. The complaint is commonly made that prayer
is impossible, because of illness or the suffering of violent
pain or a state of great weakness or langour. Did not Our
Lord pray on the cross and the martyrs on the scaffold? Actual
prayer is at such times impossible, except perhaps in ejacula-
tions or short aspirations. That is easily understood and actual
prayer is not expected of you. But let your suffering be borne
for God; suffer with submission and patience and suffer in
union with Jesus Christ and you will be offering a most excellent prayer.

A truly Christian heart then is both able to pray without
ceasing and bound to do so, partly in devoting a fixed time to
prayer and partly through its actions and sufferings. If we
consider the matter carefully, we shall see that continual
prayer is demanded by all the precepts of Christian morality.
It is indispensable for the perfect observance of those pre-

cepts, making easy that observance which, without it, would be impossible. So the two things depend on each other and the one leads to the other.

There is nothing that makes us feel the need of the interior life, the need (according to St. Paul) of being moved by the Spirit of God, more strongly than the obligation to pray continually. For we cannot fulfil this obligation if we are not constantly dependent on grace, or if we dwell voluntarily on thoughts that are opposed to, or inconsistent with, those thoughts by which God wishes our minds to be occupied moment by moment, or if we yield to affections that fill at least a part of our heart, and so deprive God of his portion. On the other hand as soon as we enter on the interior life, as soon as the Holy Spirit takes possession of our soul and governs it as he wills, the first desire that he inspires is that of continual prayer; he causes our soul to find in that practice a pleasure so intense that we become disgusted and repelled by earthly things, so that henceforward *our conversation is in heaven*.[1]

This seems a vain imagination and an extravagant degree of perfection to ordinary Christians, who through their own fault have never enjoyed this divine gift nor have ever been attracted to the inner life. It is quite enough, they say, to pray at fixed times; at other times one is allowed to give the mind a certain amount of freedom, provided it does not give way to bad thoughts, and there are a number of innocent enjoyments and attractions in which one may indulge without the least scruple. What a horrid state of bondage it would be to have to make all one's actions conform to the inward influences of grace! This continual prayer is intolerable servitude, however you like to explain it! So say the demi-Christians who find it a burden to turn to God and regard prayer as a wearisome duty. They interpret the Gospel to suit their own sentiments, instead of altering those sentiments in accordance with the clear and definite words of the Gospel.

[1] Phil. 3: 20.

They choose to deceive themselves and blaspheme things of which they are ignorant, so as to justify them in enjoying a certain amount of dissipation and giving some licence to natural desires. But these lax views can never prevail against the doctrine of Jesus Christ, and they will always find their condemnation there and in the teaching and example of the saints.

It is untrue, moreover, that the practice of continual prayer is such a galling yoke as they suggest. They appear to suppose that it must leave a man no time for the conduct of his affairs, prevent him from enjoying any social intercourse, make him seem half idiotic in conversation, with his mind always wandering, absorbed in thoughts of celestial things, and keep him, whether alone or in company, constantly serious and aloof from every kind of amusement. Human weakness could not endure such an exalted state; at all events nothing but solitary confinement could make it possible.

All this is pure exaggeration. Continual prayer is uncongenial to the senses, to the imagination, to the earthly and animal man. This I admit, and there is not a single point in the moral teaching of the Gospel that does not restrain our nature in the same way. But far from hindering a man in the performance of his duties it makes them easier, far from obstructing the use of his talents it teaches him to put them to the use for which God gave them; it makes him more energetic in his business, it enables him to bear the burden more easily and to bring everything to a successful conclusion. If it robs him of a false liberty which he idolizes and misuses to his own undoing, it leads him to the true liberty of the children of God. It does not forbid him to enjoy the social intercourse necessary and suitable to his station; on the contrary it makes him more accessible, more genial, more obliging. It allows him to take a proper share in conversation, to be lively and witty without ostentation, to be interested and even animated in manner, to talk or listen tactfully, and generally to behave so as to please everyone. He will of course always choose his

company, and in all his intercourse take care that human respect never makes him fail in charity, or in discretion, or in his
duty to God or his neighbour.

Ceaseless prayer, as I have described it, is surely a special
disposition of the heart, inclining it always toward God; it
demands no fatiguing attention of the mind, which always
remains free to apply itself to whatever God chooses or permits at any moment; but its application is given with complete detachment, so that at the first signal it passes with equal
detachment to another subject. The man who prays thus prays
without thinking, without reflection; no one knows what he is
doing, no one suffers from it. Indeed you could say that
wherever he comes he carries his prayer with him; it is never
interrupted except in sleep, and even then he may truly say
like the spouse in the Canticles: *I sleep but my heart waketh.*[1]
I do not see how a prayer of this kind can be irksome either to
oneself or to others. On the contrary I see that it is a delight to
those who practise it, that it never disturbs others and that it
is even possible to derive great profit from associating with
those who make a practice of it.

However, whether it is irksome or not, we are bidden to do
it and every Christian must put himself in the way of fulfilling
the precept.

How are we to accomplish that? We must love God, love
him with all our mind and with all our heart; everything we
do must be done for his sake with no other motive but to
please him. We must be willing to depend upon grace in everything, to acquire the agreeable habit of listening to that inward voice, to attend submissively to its warnings and be
ashamed of the slightest disobedience. We must also resolve
to deny ourselves, to battle with our self-love, to be always on
our guard against natural impulses and never to yield to them
when they interfere with our duty to God. In other words we
must be Christians in the sense of the Gospel, earnest and

[1] Song of Solomon 5: 2.

CHAPTER IX

COMMON PRAYER

Where two or three are gathered together in my name, there am I in the midst of them,[1] said Jesus Christ.

This passage has two applications.

It applies to the councils in which the chief pastors, assembled in the name of Jesus Christ, decide matters of doctrine and draw up rules of morality, and also to the assemblies of the faithful in the churches honouring God in public worship. It also applies to holy associations, formed by the faithful amongst themselves for particular objects with the approval of the Church; and, finally, it may very naturally be applied to the prayer said in common, morning and evening, in Christian families and houses and it is with this last case that I intend to treat here. At first sight it may seem unimportant, but after some consideration we shall see how far it is from being so.

Jesus Christ then declares that he is in the midst of those who come together to pray, even though there should be only two or three; and by this we must understand a special kind of presence by which he imparts to them his personal assistance, joining with them in interceding with his Father and supporting their requests with the full weight of his authority. He further promises in the same passage that all their prayers shall be granted. *If two of you shall agree on earth touching anything that they shall ask, it shall be done for them of my Father which is in heaven.*[2]

[1] Matt. 18: 20.
[2] Matt. 18: 19.

By reason then of this concerted and united prayer, what might be refused to an isolated prayer or to the personal merit of a single individual, is granted to the unanimous prayer and combined merit of several. Each prayer by itself will be weak but their union creates a force that God will not resist. Moreover, it is clear that common prayer has a merit peculiar to itself which individual prayer cannot have: that is charity, the virtue that moves the heart of God so powerfully and which he so ardently desires to establish in the hearts of men. And so it is in order to create this virtue and keep it alive amongst the faithful, that he has bestowed this privilege on united prayer.

The early Christians understood all this. In addition to the public assemblies in which all joined in the same prayer, those who lived together prayed together, husbands and wives, parents and children, masters and slaves. The custom lasted for several centuries.

But that early fervour has been relaxed so that some persons regard family prayers as a daily duty whilst others neglect them, some wish for longer prayers and others want them shorter, and a kind of devotion that seems to me ill-judged has introduced a mass of personal formulas. Even the most devout Christians have adopted the custom of praying apart and there is no harmony in families in this important matter, every individual being left to please himself.

And yet it is one of the first duties of fathers and mothers, or masters and mistresses, to contrive that their children and servants begin and end the day with prayer and to make sure that this is done. It is certain that if they fail to be watchful in this important matter and if the practice is neglected in their house, they must answer to God for it. They cannot justify themselves by saying that their children and servants are old enough to know their duty; that they had carefully instructed them in their duties, and also that they thought it a mistake to worry them and were afraid of making them hypocrites. God will not be satisfied with reasons of this kind, often put forward by persons who themselves are not very regular in their daily prayers and who, to avoid being tied to them, refuse to bind their dependents. The only way of being quite sure that this duty is performed is to arrange family prayer, to give it first place in the ordering of the household, to preside at it and insist on the attendance of every member.

But how can fathers or masters insist on establishing this practice in their homes if they themselves have abandoned it, if they do not understand its great importance and care little whether God is served and honoured in their house or not? The evil comes from themselves and it is they themselves who will suffer from it. They are not sufficiently aware that their authority comes from God, that if he is not respected or obeyed neither will they be, that vices and disorders soon appear when religion has ceased to rule and that they themselves will be the first victims. They complain every day that their children are not submissive and have no regard for their advice, that they are disobedient and disgrace them by their conduct; that their servants are lazy, careless, heartless and disloyal. There they are right but they do not trace the evil to its source, having no idea that the origin of the disorder is the absence of religion and that they themselves are the cause of it by their speech, their example and their complete indifference to everything that has to do with the worship of God. Let them put into practice what I have suggested and they will reap the fruits and their complaints will cease.

Even if they had grounds for their belief that everyone said his prayers in private, there would still be the loss of general edification, which is a duty that all the members of a family owe to each other.

Indeed it cannot be doubted that prayers are said better together. People adopt a more decorous posture, there is an observance of mutual respect, and nobody takes there the sort of liberties in which anyone might freely indulge when prayer is private. As a rule they pay more attention, the devotion of some inspires and encourages others and if the head of the family himself recites the prayers, his serious manner and his earnest devout tone of voice make an impression on all the company. Leave children and servants to their own devices and often they will not pray at all, or they will say only one short and hasty prayer. The young, especially, need the inspiration of authority and example; they easily yield to the temptation of omitting their religious duties, when there is no one to see them and guide them. In the morning laziness keeps the household in bed; a servant arises only when his duties call him; afterwards there is never an interval for prayer. At night he is overpowered by sleep and as soon as he retires, goes to bed without a thought of prayer. No habit is more easily formed and when once it has been formed it is difficult to correct it.

The benefits that result from united prayer in families are countless and of the greatest importance.

It contributes more than anything else to love and respect between husband and wife, to the holy use of wedlock and to mutual kindness, support and confidence. Whatever may be said to the contrary, men have no rooted esteem and love for one another, nor do they confide and trust in each other, except when they possess and recognize in each other a feeling for religion. What surer guarantee can there be for these religious sentiments than harmony and agreement in the service of God?

It keeps alive in father and mother the loftiest ideal of their holy estate and the importance of their duties with regard to their children's education. It makes them carry out these duties faithfully and with attentive care for the smallest details. It draws down the graces they need. Indeed they need these graces every moment if they are to mould the minds and hearts of their children, if they are not to be discouraged by their characteristic faults or daunted by the laborious unremitting care they demand. They must be cautious lest severity or indulgence go too far; they must beware lest familiarity should diminish the respect that is due, or that the exercise of authority should suppress natural affection, and they must love them all equally or at any rate show no marked preference, so often the cause of jealousy and hatred.

It gives children a kind of religious veneration of their parents; it disposes their minds to give more attention to parental advice and bends their wills to more complete obedience. There is nothing more likely to lead children to fear God in the person of their parents than a high opinion of their piety. How can they acquire that opinion except by seeing their parents at prayer? The love for their parents that God has implanted in the hearts of children, is increased by their faith in their goodness more than one can believe. The natural feelings are thus heightened and perfected by grace and gain greater strength, greater stability, greater depth. Here is a religious family and there is an irreligious one; what a difference there is between them! On the one hand we see obedience, peace and unity; on the other hand self-sufficiency, restlessness and discord. It is piety that makes the first so happy, whilst the second is made wretched by its self-sufficiency. It is impossible that the members of a family which recites morning and evening prayer together, regularly and reverently, should fail to behave like good Christians in every other way, impossible that God should not watch over them with special care so that their happiness is secure. On the contrary, in families where the practice is neglected, it is common enough to find that all, or at any rate many, of their members omit altogether even their private prayers and in a house like this there is no religion at all. God does not dwell there and, whatever the appearances, every member is more or less unhappy, husband and wife, parents and children, being a constant source of trouble to each other.

Another ancient custom that died out with family prayers,

was that every evening before retiring the children asked their father for a blessing; a custom entirely admirable whose origin may be traced back to the early days of the Church and even to the time of the patriarchs, a custom that Scripture permits us to regard as a divine institution, admirably adapted to encourage in children a spirit of simplicity and respect for their parents. If it could only be revived to-day and children would submit to it as a religious principle, as long as they lived in their father's house and under his authority, what a change there would be in our general behaviour! It was not for nothing that God attached so much weight to the blessing and curse of a father. Noah blessed Shem and Japheth and cursed Ham. The effect of his words extended over all their posterity, that is to say the whole human race. Jacob by an act of divine providence, the secret of which had been revealed to Rebecca, secured the blessing that Isaac had intended for Esau, and Esau's descendants were less favoured by God than those of his brother and were nearly always subject to them. When Jacob was dying Joseph brought his two sons to his father, who purposely crossed his arms and laid his right hand on Ephraim the younger of the two, and Ephraim's tribe became the largest and most powerful after Judah. The blessings given by Jacob to his own twelve sons, were so many prophecies which were afterwards fulfilled in the twelve tribes. Apart from the solemnity of this ancient benediction, God has always looked with favour on the prayer of parents thus expressed and, when a child begs his father with faith to bless him, he always receives in answer the grace of the Most High.

Prayer in common would be equally profitable to masters and mistresses as to servants. Masters would be treated with more consideration, being more beloved and better served. Servants for their part would have greater confidence in their masters; they would be more kindly treated, and would not have to endure the haughtiness and severity which make them sensible of the humiliation of their position. Masters, who were in the habit of praying with them, would remember at their prayers that differences of rank are nothing in the sight of God, that in his eyes men are only distinguished by their piety, and that he perhaps considers them less important than the least of their servants. This thought recurring twice a day, would have its effect on the rest of their conduct and make them more human and accessible. The servants at the same time would learn in these moments of prayer to see God in their masters, and respect in them the authority that is derived from him; they would serve them with increasing zeal, affection and fidelity as their attitude became more spiritual, elevated and disinterested.

The hour when the family or household was assembled for prayer would be the best time for reading aloud some edifying and instructive book. If such reading only lasted a quarter of an hour each day, it would sow seeds of piety in the hearts of the children and servants which would later bear fruit.

Experience only can show what blessings God would delight to shower on a household in which he was thus honoured. Sooner or later every vice would be banished from it and every virtue would flourish under its roof. The most perfect order would reign in it; all who dwelt there would conspire to make life happy and joyous for each other. To the exercises I have suggested I would add the habit of thanksgiving in common before and after meals, a very ancient and holy custom that was once in use, but has now been abandoned in nearly every family. These things are apparently very trifling matters, yet nevertheless it is upon such small things that the hallowing of every private house depends, and therefore that of the town and of the whole State. The proof of this is to note how the neglect, omission and scorn of these same exercises have introduced licence, the spirit of impiety, first into families, then into towns and finally into whole kingdoms.

What reasons can be given to absolve heads of families

from the duty of introducing such customs into their households?

Can you say that solid piety does not depend on such trifles? Common sense forbids us to speak in that way, for facts prove the contrary to be true. Can we say that the world has abandoned such customs and that a revival of them would court ridicule? It is just because the world has abandoned them that the Christian ought to restore them, and if a man feels himself incapable of facing ridicule he is unworthy of being called a Christian.

Perhaps you will say that such practices mean that one is subjected to a strict rule of life, so that the household must be ordered in the manner of a monastery with fixed hours for religious exercises and therefore for rising and going to bed What inconvenience is there in this? Would not everyone agree that of all habits the most useful in every way is to regulate our time, and especially the beginning and end of the day which are the two fixed points on which the whole sequence of our actions depends? If I were to reply that the habit of rising late and going late to rest, of turning day into night and night into day, had contributed more than anything else to the weakening and even extinction of piety, I should be uttering a great and melancholy truth.

As for the habits of monasteries which the world makes such a point of avoiding, the truth is that these practices were originally the rule in Christian families and were from them continued in the cloisters.

"But the arrangement of my establishment does not lend itself to the introduction of these practices." So much the worse; that means that it is worthless and ought to be reformed. Everything that makes it impossible for you, your children and your servants, to fulfil these ordinary duties of religion, ought to be abolished or altered; there is no room for hesitation.

"But how can I impose this practice on children who are

grown up or servants who are unwilling to join in them? They will grumble and laugh behind my back and refuse to obey me." If you were a truly Christian father or master, these alleged difficulties would not stand in your way; you would hardly give a thought to them, for human respect would not affect you. Begin by making an open profession of your religion; after a time, when no one can doubt your sincerity, express your desire to institute family prayers and explain your reasons; say that you are moved to do this by your conscience and feel bound to take this step; fix a day when you will begin, choosing some important festival. I doubt if your children will oppose you, still less your servants. You do not know how strong a hold religion has on men's hearts. As for any murmurs of opposition or ridicule, despise them; they will soon cease. Make it clear that you do not wish to force anyone, but that you will be pleased with those who fall in with your wishes. Most of the household will join in the prayers, you may be sure, even from the very first; the rest will follow their example to avoid being conspicuous, and in a few days' time you will have them also. Make the attempt and count on God to further your pious intentions.

O my God, were it only to force myself to be regular in performing so holy a duty, I will establish the practice of common prayer in my family and household. But in addition I owe an example to my children and servants, and I owe it to myself to make sure that they pay thee the daily homage that is thy due. I am a father and a master of a household; if these two titles, under which I am thy representative, give me rights they also prescribe duties, the most important of which is to see that my dependents serve thee; it is right that I should use it in bringing honour to thee.

Pardon me, Lord, for my past negligencies in this regard. I am resolved to repair them. I may have been a cause of scandal to my household; I would fain be a cause of edification. I

G

must answer to thee for the conduct of my children and servants and it concerns my salvation that I should give a good account of them to thee. Let thy blessing rest on the resolution that I make to persevere, and grant me grace to be faithful to it all the days of my life. Amen.

CHAPTER X

THE LORD'S PRAYER

When the Apostles, inspired by the Holy Christ, asked the
Saviour to teach them to pray, he gave them the Dominical
Prayer which we call the Lord's Prayer: a divine prayer,
whether we think of its author or the sentiments it expresses.
It is a prayer that Jesus Christ has taught to all of us in the
persons of his Apostles, a prayer that the Church has always
placed above all others, which makes an essential part of the
sacrifice of our altars where it is never omitted; it is a prayer
by which she begins all her offices, which she teaches to children of the tenderest age, explains to them in all her catechisms
and recommends to the faithful for continual use several
times a day and especially in the morning and evening.

This prayer in short contains everything. Jesus Christ who
knew our duties and needs has expressed them all in the
fewest of words. A Christian can say nothing in praise of God
or ask him for anything which is not contained in it. Its
simplicity makes its meaning plain to everybody; its sublimity
of thought is beyond the capacity of the greatest genius; to
comprehend its full meaning we need a supernatural light.
But like all prayer it is meant for the heart rather than the
mind and whilst it is necessary to understand it, it is infinitely
more important to feel it.

Jesus Christ's intention in teaching it to us cannot have
been that we should merely recite it with our lips; he meant
us to grasp it with our mind, to appropriate its sentiments and
make it our rule of conduct. There is no Christian anywhere
who does not know it by heart, for it is the chief prayer and

the most ordinary prayer. But do we understand it and have we fathomed its meaning? Have we ever asked the Saviour to open our minds so that we may try to understand it? There are not many Christians even amongst the most pious who are humble enough to admit that they do not understand the Paternoster and sufficiently enlightened by God to recognize that it can only be understood by the truly spiritual and only when the Spirit who gave it himself gives the explanation.

But even this is not the whole root of the matter. Do we not recite the prayer mechanically and merely from habit? Do we feel it with our hearts and is it the expression of our deepest feelings? Can we say at each word, each phrase: That is what I think, that is what I feel, that is what I desire? If the sentiments it expresses are not constantly present in our hearts, we cannot flatter ourselves that we are true Christians.

Do we believe moreover that the *Paternoster* is not only the most perfect rule of conduct we can have, but also the most indispensable? Do we believe that it is the summary of the Gospel, the very essence of all that is most perfect in the moral teaching of Jesus Christ? And do we, as a matter of fact, think, speak and act in conformity with this prayer? Can our life bear comparison with it? I could wish every Christian to ask himself these questions seriously. Why do we pray? In order to live rightly. What do we ask in this prayer? How we ought to live. This is not a prayer composed by men to help us in our devotion. It is Jesus Christ who gave it to us and made it to suit his own purposes and not ours. When he said, *Thus you shall pray*, he was in effect saying to us: You shall regulate your lives according to this prayer. If we fail to do this we shall be condemned out of our own mouths. Every day you prayed for these things, he will say, and your conduct gave the lie to your prayers; you never dreamt that there was a vital connexion between your prayers and your actions.

Since it is certain that we shall be judged one day by Jesus

Christ in accordance with this prayer called by his name, let us spend a few moments in trying to understand its meaning and in pondering the obligations that it imposes on us.

It is with this end in view that I am going to attempt this explanation under the guidance of grace, never forgetting that I am working on my own behalf no less, and indeed more, than on yours.

OUR FATHER

It is to my father that I am speaking.

I should never have dared, sinner that I am, to give this name to God, nor to call myself his child. It is Jesus Christ who gives me the courage to do so. He begins by reminding me that grace has made me the child of God; that I am his child by adoption and have been raised to this glorious privilege by the unspeakable mystery of the union of the Word with his sacred humanity. As man Jesus Christ is my brother; after his resurrection he called his disciples by this name and he called us all his disciples. In the Gospel he always says, *My Father*, and, *Your Father*, placing us, as it were, in the same rank and degree of relationship to his God as himself, not only authorizing us but even obliging us to share his privileges and rights.

Now let us go further back and consider from the beginning and in all its consequences what the divine fatherhood means for us.

God is my father by creation.

I derive my whole being from him. My parents' share in the life of my body should count almost for nothing; they were only the instruments through which my life came, as they followed the laws laid down by God's will. It was he who created the material of my body and moulded it in my mother's womb, designed its form and endowed it with the principle of life and movement, provided its nourishment and inspired its growth. How much more then is he my father than those who gave me birth. If I owe respect and love and obedience to them how much more do I owe all these to God, whose rights over the work of his hands have a deeper foundation and a larger sphere.

It is a small matter that he is the creator and architect of that least part of my being. My soul, that substance which is free, intelligent and immortal in its nature, is derived altogether from him. My parents contributed nothing to its existence; at the most they ignorantly determined the moment of its creation. My soul, then, has in reality no father but God, to whom it owes its being, its properties and its qualities. He made it what it is because he willed to do so out of pure goodness, having no need to do so and being perfectly happy in his complete independence. Here indeed is a title to fatherhood far beyond any earthly one.

In addition to this there is another important difference. In so far as I owe my existence to my parents they gave it me by a fleeting action. It was not in their power to preserve it, and in spite of all their tenderness and all their care they might have seen me deprived of it at any moment. On the other hand the action whereby God created me always goes on, and if it ceased for a single moment my body and soul would fall again into nothingness. Not only then is he my father but he continues to be so perpetually. He preserves my bodily life until my last breath; after my death he still preserves the life of my soul, and when he has re-united body and soul at the general resurrection he will preserve them both throughout eternity. Therefore he has been, he is, and he will continue to be my father as long as I have any existence; and my soul will for ever exist either by itself, or joined to the body, or re-united to it. My dependence on him for my existence being so great and the benefits of his fatherhood so constant, what ought then my love for him to be? What shall be my gratitude?

Something more I must say. Whatever be God's relationship to me in the order of nature, it is a small matter compared with what he is in the order of grace, where he manifests himself as my father in a much more excellent way.

In creating me he gave me no doubt a great gift, the primary gift on which rests all his other gifts. It is a gift that could only come from a Being of infinite power, goodness and generosity. But to have created me as an object of his love and favour, to have enriched my soul from the very beginning with supernatural gifts, to have destined it to possess and love him and enjoy his own happiness eternally, is a new kind of gift that is infinitely superior to the first. I, who am the child of God by birth, am his child in a much more exalted sense and in a much more intimate way, because of my destiny which draws me near to him, unites me inseparably to him and makes of him and myself in truth one single being, having only one will and enjoying the same privileges.

Such a destiny was far from being my due. I could have been deprived of it without having any cause for complaint; I should not have known that I was capable of enjoying it unless God had revealed it to me.

Earthly fathers do not give their children full possession of their property until they die. The children only acquire it by the right of accession and inheritance, and they gain greater wealth only by losing what is dearest to them. Nothing is given to them; they are only left what can no longer be kept by their parents, who would have kept the capital at least as long as they continued to live. It is not so with our heavenly Father who, since he cannot die, has nothing to leave us afterwards. He longs to give us all that he has and all that he is, and he meant to give us eternal life, after this short probation of a temporal life which would itself have been happy but for the coming of sin. To attain this second life we were not even to pass through the gate of death. Such was our original state.

Could the fatherly goodness of God have gone further than this? Has he not done more to deserve our love than we could have dared to hope for, more than we could have dreamed of desiring?

Yet here is a mark of fatherly love still more wonderful.

The human race, though endowed with so many gifts and destined for such bliss, played false from the very beginning. The first man and woman rebelled against their Creator and Father, and through the most insane pride disobeyed his commands in the hope that their transgression would make them his equals. Behold them with all their progeny deprived for ever of the privileges of their state. Behold them deserving nothing but God's everlasting hatred and punishment. They had no hope but in his mercy. But he had foreseen the evil and provided the remedy for it and, O my God, what a remedy! Could it have been hoped for from any father but thee? He who is in himself eternally fecund possessed an only Son equal to himself, and he dedicated him to the salvation of mankind. He sent him to the earth, clothed with our own guilty and degraded nature, and by a decree fixed from all eternity ordained that in that nature he should be humiliated, should suffer, should die for us and thus expiate, a willing victim, both the first sin and all the other sins that sprang from it.

Adopted in this Son, *first-born of all creatures*, men are now restored with interest to the position and rights of Children of God. The heaven once closed through their own sin is again opened to them; assistance more abundant and effectual is given them to rise thither, and though incapable themselves of any merit, they may hope all things and aspire to all things through the merits now become theirs of the God-Man.

Thus has the Father loved the rebels and ingrates so as to offer up and sacrifice for them the object of his eternal tenderness. Let us silently adore and love the best of fathers and consecrate ourselves to his glory!

I would wish to drive home the consideration of the fatherly love of God for us.

By whom was this sentence, passed in our favour against the dear Son, to be carried out? No doubt by the devils, who, condemned irrevocably to the torments of hell, had become God's irreconcilable enemies? Not at all. The devils were only the instigators of men and it was the men themselves who denied, insulted and killed the Son of God who came to save them. The blow was delivered there where one could least have expected it, by a nation chosen by a special providence, by a nation to whom God had chosen to be Legislator and King, by a nation to whom he had sent a long line of prophets to announce the coming of the world's Liberator. In any case, the crime that this nation committed would have been committed by any other nation in the same position. For on what argument and in what way could we suppose ourselves to be better than the Jews? We should have been God-killers as they were and no other proof of this is needed than the sins by which we crucify the Son of God afresh.

It is then true that God in his incomprehensible goodness has used for the salvation of the human race the most execrable crime ever committed by the human race; he foresaw the crime and knew that it would be renewed age after age by all the sinners of the earth.

These mercies of our heavenly Father of which I have been speaking are not so universal that they cannot be personal to each one of us. Every time we utter those first words of the Lord's Prayer, *Our Father*, we should have in our minds a vague idea at least of this meaning and our hearts should glow with the most lively and ardent affection. Otherwise we are saying them only with our lips without any intelligent thought.

But there are also countless benefits that are peculiar and personal to ourselves, so many sins so often forgiven, so many graces granted, so many kindnesses and tender appeals, such patience in suffering our delays, such forbearance in prolonging our sinful life, when it might have been cut short in the hour of our first sin and no time left for our repentance.

We ought, each of us, to call to mind all that we owe to God and remind ourselves of it when we say *Our Father*. The very thought will surely fill us with rapturous adoration; we shall fall prostrate in an ecstasy of love and gratitude before the vision of his sublime charity. The one word, *Father*, will furnish us with thoughts and affections enough to occupy us for a lifetime. No meditation could exhaust its depth of meaning, no contemplation reach the height of this thought; after we have fed our souls with it on earth we shall find in heaven sufficient matter for praise, benediction and thanksgiving.

I have not however said everything for I have still to speak of what the Father is in himself, of his nature and infinite perfections. Here again are depths where the mind loses itself and where the heart discovers still stronger and purer motives for loving him.

If *the glory of children are their fathers*,[1] what glory is ours. What triumph and joy are on the thought: I have God himself for Father! What a noble pride should this inspire in me, what contempt and loathing for all that can make me unworthy of my high origin!

O my Father, how greatly I am ennobled when I raise myself above the things of earth and remember that thou art God, that thou dost exist by the necessity of thy nature, that thou art infinitely perfect, sovereign Being, eternal, measureless, self-subsistent; that I belong to thee, that I am thy child and that thou gloriest in this. May I not glory in it too? May I not say: O how happy I am in having such a Father! In thee what majesty, what beauty, what wealth, what knowledge, what holiness, what joy! I greatly rejoice that I can understand nothing of the unspeakable wonder of thy attributes, for, if the sublimest intellect created was able to conceive of thee, thou wouldst not be what thou art nor wouldst thou dwell in light inaccessible.

Prov. 17: 6.

How perfect is the union and yet how complete the distinction between the three adorable persons who possess in thee the same nature without loss of unity. Divine Fatherhood, who can understand thee? Eternal Sonship, who can explain thee? Essential love of Father and Son, Holy Spirit, who can comprehend thy Procession from both? This Unity and Trinity, the incommunicable property of thy nature is my glory, my joy and my bliss, because it is thine. Thou art my Father and the child is noble with all the nobility of his father, rich with all his riches, perfect with all his perfection. Thus it is with me by thy will, as far as it is possible to me; and this it ought to be by my own will also, if I love thee and love myself in thee as I should.

Name of all delight, why have I been able to use it so often without a thought of what it meant, without being overcome with trust and gratitude? My Saviour and my master, I appeal to thee to teach me to utter this name of *Father* as I ought. Grant that whenever it is on my lips there may be in mind a prayer, so sweet and so profound that it cannot find utterance in words. What need is there of words? Is not everything expressed in these first words? When I have spoken them with the lips of my heart I have said all and my Father has heard all.

OUR FATHER

Observe that Jesus Christ has not taught us to say *My Father;* he commands us to say *Our Father*. He does not wish us to use his prayer in our own individual name, but he composed it from beginning to end in such a way that we should speak in the name of all the brother-Christians, whose Father God is, no less than he is ours. Just as the word *Father* contains all the reasons for loving God, so the words, *Our Father*, contain all the reasons for loving our neighbour.

For since God is the father of all men he loves them all and consequently wishes them to love one another. To fail in love towards our neighbour is to fail in love towards God; because in loving God we pledge ourselves to love all that he loves, and for the same reasons and for the same object, since love as it exists in God is essentially the pattern and model for our own love. His fatherly love prompts him to do good to all men, to desire their salvation and supply them with the necessary means according to the designs of his Providence. We have the same duties to fulfil towards one another in temporal matters as well as in spiritual. It is not enough to abstain from harming one another; every man must wish well to his neighbour and do good to him on every opportunity as far as possible; he must desire his salvation and work for it by his prayer, speech and example.

Let us develop this thought further and find in the divine fatherhood the motives for loving our fellows.

Since God, if we regard him only as Creator, is our common Father, we are all brothers as we are all his creatures, and this natural relationship should lead us all to love one another.

According to the flesh we have a common origin; we make up only one great family which includes every age and every region. You may say that if we trace our descent to our first parents we shall find our relationship very remote, and that love founded on such a tie must be extremely weak, since even brothers and sisters have often no love for each other. I admit it but I maintain none the less that God intended this primal link to unite us all, however loosely knit we may think it to be.

For the remoteness of our bodily relationship we have some compensation in the close connexion between our souls. These all issue directly from God at the first moment of our lives; in this way the generations that are alive at the same time have a real fraternal tie, and they stand, so to speak, in the first degree of relationship.

If in addition our destiny is the same, if we are called by our Father to the same inheritance, if we hope one day to be united in the same fatherland and eternally to enjoy the same happiness; then here indeed is a very cogent reason for mutual love, since we are citizens of the same city, co-heirs of the same lands, which we shall share without dispute or rather which will be the common property of each one of us. We are like travellers bound all for the same destination where, once arrived, divine love will make us one in heart and soul. Why should we hate each other and quarrel and hurt one another during the journey? Is that likely to make us love each other when we are all together in our Father's house? If harmony is to reign amongst us then it is evident that it must begin in this life. Would we wish to leave this world full of feelings which will banish us from the region where God's children, perfected and in some way merged in the divine unity and free from envy and jealousy, will be happy, not only in their own joy but in the joy of others. O heavenly country, our soul's native land, centre of all brotherly love and final end of our common hope, how can Christians love thee, long for thee and strive to find in thee their rest, without being united on earth in the closest bonds of charity? What after all is this Fatherland? It is our Father Himself. There he is everything, he does everything and for those who dwell there he is their all. It is inconceivable that children running eagerly to greet the same father, who long to enjoy his caresses, who ought to draw nearer together as they draw nearer to him, it is inconceivable, I say, that they should become so deeply estranged as not to be able to endure each other and should even wish each other ill. And for what reason? For nothing but base temporal interests which are a hindrance to them on their journey and would, unless they could free themselves from them, keep them for ever from their goal.

But if, over and above what I have just said, the heavenly Father has made us all his children in His only Son, so that in his eyes we make only one person with the Son and he extends to us the love which he has for his Son, if he has redeemed us all by the death of that Son, washed us and purified us in his blood, fed us with his flesh which is inseparably united with the Divinity; if he has heaped favours upon us for his Son's sake and if that same Son, become our brother, burns with divine love for us, so that his great desire, the one commandment peculiar to his own law, sealed with his blood, is that we should love one another as he has loved us and as his Father loves us in Him; then what other motive more powerful than these can there be for loving each other with mutual charity? Your neighbour may or may not be lovable in himself; that is not what you have to consider. The natural qualities of mind and heart contribute nothing to supernatural love, which springs from a higher source. What claim had your neighbour to be loved when God's glance rested on him? What claim had you yourself? Answer me that. The man whom God thinks worthy of his love, you do not think worthy of yours. Because you do not love him, do you think that God should cease to love him? Do you not see that you are giving judgment against yourself and authorizing God to reject you on the same grounds on which you reject your brother?

"But the man you wish me to love does not love me, he speaks ill of me, he wishes to injure me, he has even done me grievous harm." But does his failure to do his duty excuse you from doing yours? It is not in your neighbour's feelings and behaviour towards you that you should seek reasons for loving or hating him. If that is what nature says, what does grace say? And when it is a question of brotherly love you must pay no attention to nature. What would be your fate, miserable child, if your Father before loving you had made enquiry into your feelings and conduct towards him? What were you like when he adopted you and what have you been like since? Your offences, most serious and often repeated, have they induced him to cast you off? And you disown your brother and break all the ties of charity that bind you to him. And you think that you have the right to do this because he has injured you. You will be condemned out of your own mouth and your Father will judge you by the same rule you follow in judging others.

The two great commandments on which hang all the law and the prophets are contained then in the first two words of the Lord's Prayer, and a Christian should never say *Our Father* without feeling an awakening of the love of God and his neighbour and all the reasons for it.

Do the words produce this effect on ourselves?

I do not ask that all you have just read should come into your mind every time you recite the Paternoster. That is neither possible nor necessary. It is enough that you grasped it once for all and that you should intend to remain in the frame of mind demanded by these words. Is that true for you? Are you striving seriously to make it true? Are you continually asking God to help you to that end?

Have you ever thought of questioning yourself on this important matter in some such way as this: Am I fit, am I worthy to utter the words, *Our Father?* Do I love God, do I love my neighbour enough for that? If I am in a state of mortal sin how dare I call God my father since I have neither contrition for my sin nor the desire to abandon it? How can the Holy Spirit say *Father* when I have chased him from my heart? If I hate my brother, if I wish him ill, if I have a secret joy when evil comes to him, if I bring malicious judgments and intemperate language to bear on his faults and vices, perhaps even on his good qualities and virtues, if I hear him slandered with pleasure and if I invite others to abuse him, how can I have the face to say to God, *Our Father?* Do I see in him the Father of that neighbour whom I detest and tear to pieces? Do I recognize him as my own Father when my feelings are so opposed to his? Has no St. Paul declared that it is the Spirit of adoption, the Spirit of love, which speaks in us and bids us cry, *Father*, *Father?* Does he dwell in me, does he pray in me, if I do not love my brother?

I am willing to grant that your state of mind is not absolutely wicked. But in regard to God it is a state of lukewarmness and slackness; in regard to your neighbour a state, at all events for the time, of resentment and suspicion, indifference and insensibility. Is it possible for you to say *Our Father* as Jesus Christ wished you to say it?

You will understand me: the firm intention to keep ourselves constantly in a fit state to utter these words as a Child of God ought to utter them, is itself sufficient to sanctify us, because we shall then allow nothing into our hearts that can wound however slightly the love of God and love of our neighbour.

OUR FATHER WHICH ART IN HEAVEN

Our Father is in heaven and we are on the earth. Sad and painful separation of a heart that loves.

The heart would be inconsolable if it did not know that such is God's will and that the separation will only last for a time, after which the children will be united together in the father's house.

Since heaven is my Father's home it must be my true Fatherland, for that word *Fatherland* means the country of the father. Therefore I am a stranger on earth; it is for me only a temporary dwelling-place. God keeps me here on probation in order that by my faith, my ardent longing, and my faithful obedience to him, I may desire to be summoned to himself and given a place near him in heaven, whence my soul derives its origin and whither it should aspire to return. This soul of mine is entirely spiritual and has nothing in common with corporeal nature. Earthly objects are unworthy of its care and affection; it has no need of them for itself, and if it should sometimes seek to possess them, it is for the sake of the body to which it is united and of the fleeting human life which is the result of that union.

But what is the heaven which is God's dwelling-place?

Is it the blue vault sown with stars which we see over our heads and which the Scriptures call the *firmament?* No, it was incorrectly, and only to accommodate themselves to our ideas, that the Holy Books have represented the firmament and the sky as God's palace and habitation. Since it is removed from the earth at a vast distance and its mighty curve is of a magnitude inconceivable, whilst, except for the stars that glow within it, our eyes see it as an empty space; since a changeless order pervades the movement of the heavenly bodies and among them all is harmony, silence and apparent peace; since, when we look at it, our imagination raises us above all earthly things, detaching our soul from the body, as it were, and transporting it to the realm of peace; for all these reasons it is a natural image of the intellectual heaven where God dwells and it is useful in giving us a picture which conforms to our human way of seeing things, into which natural things always enter.

Heaven, to speak correctly, is God, it stands for his immensity. There is not, there could not be, any other place for Him than Himself and when we say *Our Father which art in Heaven* it is as though we were to say: Our Father who dost exist and dwell within Thyself, whose pure but infinite substance fills all things, and within whom as in a space without measure and bounds all created things subsist. When the impious scoffer asks: What is Heaven and where is Heaven? he places himself amongst the ignorant and boorish crowd; if he does not understand the truth it is a want of intelligence, but if he is pretending not to understand then he is malicious.

I am, then, in this present moment, existing in this immensity of God, for where else could I exist? But I am not in Him as I shall be or as I hope to be some day. Even here I know God, though very imperfectly. I think of him, but my thoughts are continually distracted by my requirements, my business and the objects that surround me. I love him but my love is never absolutely pure, for my will is perpetually subject to other in-

H

fluences. I possess him but I do so more by hope than experience, and this possession that I have by faith may be lost at any time by my own fault. In the other life it will not be so. What the life of my soul will be in the divine immensity I can neither explain nor understand. But I know that I shall see God, that is to say, I shall know him with the whole capacity of my understanding, according to the degree of glory that my soul merits. I know that I shall be for ever occupied in the contemplation of God and that no other thought or need or interest or object will distract my attention from him. I know that I shall love him with all the strength of my will, with a love that can never again be diverted or shared or weakened. I know that I shall possess God in a close and direct union, with the certainty of never being parted from him. These are the chief differences between my present temporary state and my future state which will have no end.

As for the heaven which will be the dwelling place of glorified bodies after the resurrection, Scripture teaches us that when the heaven and earth we see now have been consumed by fire, God will form *new heavens* and a *new earth*, which will share the qualities of the bodies clothed in glory and will have a natural affinity with them.

How many reasons then have I to long for Heaven, my true fatherland, the abode of bliss where the Father awaits me to welcome me and show me the place he has prepared for me! How can I utter the words, *Our Father which art in Heaven*, without lifting up my heart to him with the most ardent longing, and without tearing my thoughts from the things of this life which hold me back and prevent me from taking flight? Since my Father is in Heaven, how can I indulge myself on the earth, how can I seek imaginary happiness so far from Him? All I can do is to submit to his will. It is he who has consigned me to this gloomy prison for a time, how long He only knows. He has placed me here on purpose to test my obedience and love, because he wishes my everlasting habitation in his house to be a reward attained in virtue of merit. On his side it is a gift, a favour to which I had never a right; on my side it must be an acquisition, a victory; I must take the greatest care to value it at its true worth, to long for it, to spare no effort to obtain it and to despise and shun and detest everything that can turn my thoughts and affections in any other direction.

How wretched I should be if, when I am beset with every kind of evil, surrounded by objects that cannot truly satisfy the needs of my soul, surrounded by false pleasures, false honours, false riches; if, when I am a burden to myself and a victim of the injustice of men, I were not sustained by the consoling vision of the real benefits, the unmixed joys, the sure and permanent possessions that my Father offers me and that I shall never find except in his presence. *Alas*, I might at any moment cry, how long is my pilgrimage? *What a stranger is my soul* in this place of exile! What a weary and dangerous voyage on the stormy seas of this world! When shall I descry, even in the distance, the haven of my fatherland? When shall I arrive there? When shall I enjoy its perfect security?

Till now the remembrance of death has filled me with terror because I never considered the deepest desires of my soul nor the teachings of religion. But now, far from dreading death, I await it with godly impatience. It will be the end of my sad journeying and the beginning and gateway of my happiness. It is death that will open for me the door of my Father's house and take me in. What after all is this life from which I find it so hard to break loose? It is a banishment, a long and wearisome captivity. Does not the exile who drags his sorrow from country to country receive the news of his recall with rapture? Does a prisoner feel himself aggrieved when his chains are broken, his cell is thrown open and he is restored to the light of the sun? Ah, let it come soon, the hour when I shall see again my fatherland, and my father will fold me in his arms and I shall enjoy to the full and for ever the sweet liberty of his children.

Are these your feelings, my fellow Christians? Has your frequent repetition of the *Pater* inspired you with this longing? Of what use then has the divine prayer been to you if it has not kindled in you the desire for Heaven, if you still cling to earth, if you cherish every tie that binds you to it, if every day you multiply and tighten those bonds, if you base your happiness on earth, if you know only the uncertain joys of earth and would without a single regret sacrifice to them the bliss of eternity? If this is your state say no more, *Our Father which art in Heaven.* You no longer regard God as your Father, nor his abode, home of glory and immortality, as your Fatherland. Shame and humiliation and confusion should overwhelm your ignoble hearts, ungrateful and unnatural children that you are. You are unworthy of the joy your Father has laid up for you, and you will force him to exclude you for ever unless your hearts are changed.

HALLOWED BE THY NAME

To speak truly, God has no name.

Before he created anything He existed alone and since the creation he has been alone in a sense, for he has neither genus nor species. His unique and incommunicable nature sufficiently distinguishes him from all that is not He. However, he was graciously pleased to give himself a name when he made himself known to mankind and announced to Moses that his name was *Jehovah*, i.e. *He who is.* This name being infinitely holy in itself has no need of being hallowed, and indeed could not possibly be so, since it is superior to all sanctification. Moreover by whom could it be sanctified?

What then do we desire for God when we say, *Hallowed by thy name?* We desire that all men should know him, adore him, love him, obey him and render to him all the glory that is his due.

It is only right and even natural that a child should be jealous for his father's honour and desire him to be glorified;

that he should delight in his glory and contribute to it all that he can.

But if this wish that we express on God's behalf be sincere, it is evident that the first thing we have to do is to hallow his Name ourselves. That is where we must begin. The desire that others should glorify him is only a result of our determination to glorify him ourselves. If we do nothing for God's glory, if it be not the first intention of all our prayers and the chief aim of our actions, if we hardly think of it even and consider only our own interests in our worship of God, it is almost a mockery to say to him: *Hallowed be thy name*. Being so cold and negligent in glorifying him ourselves, we must undoubtedly be still more indifferent with regard to the honour owed to him by others.

What obligations then does this zeal for the hallowing of God's name lay upon me?

First of all it binds me to hallow it in my own person by consecrating to the glory of God my whole being, my thoughts affections and actions; not only by abstaining from anything that could in any way dishonour him, but also by neglecting no opportunity of glorifying him. If I behave in this way to God I may believe that I am not using empty words when I say, *Hallowed be thy name*, and that I feel in my heart what my lips express. For I cannot really strive to glorify God in this way unless I aspire to love him with a genuine love, the reality of the love consisting, first of all and above all, in considering the interests of the beloved person.

But if I aspire to love God in this way, it is impossible that I should not desire him to be loved and glorified by other men also, since all men owe him the homage which is due from me. This desire will prompt me to work to this end with all my strength, according to my condition and opportunities. It will lead me to ask God in what way he wishes me to advance his glory, and to co-operate earnestly with his purpose for my life. It will lead me to understand that I only live on the earth with the talents, influence and authority that I have, in order to bring honour to God, and that every other use I make of my time, liberty and possessions is a sheer waste.

My first care then will be to see that he is glorified by those who are directly dependent on me, my wife, children and servants. If I am a person of rank or hold important positions in town or country, in the army or State, I shall employ all my influence and power to maintain the observance of God's commandments and those of his Church, and the respect due to his religion, his churches and ministers. I shall expose every form of scandal with all my power, and shall not allow those who are guilty to go unpunished.

Everyone may know his obligations in this respect; they extend to everything he is responsible for doing or preventing in virtue of his position or office.

If such is the zeal for God's glory required of the ordinary Christian, what should be expected of bishops, priests, heads of communities, preachers and confessors, the special object of whose ministry is the hallowing of God's name? It is for that alone that he has endowed them with their sacred office, for that that they have been specially set apart. They are responsible to him for the promotion of his glory, which according to his holy will was to be advanced through them, and he will demand from them a strict account.

Every day we say to God, *Hallowed be thy name*.

Which of us strives to hallow that name himself, to hallow it as much as he can, as much as God desires and expects? That is the rule and measure of our duty. Every omission and negligence in this matter is blameworthy, and what an enormous field this covers! Let us judge its extent by the words of St. Paul: *Do all to the glory of God*, for he includes expressly eating and drinking and makes no exception whatever. This is not merely a counsel, but a precept that concerns every Christian. Ah, would his holy name be profaned, outraged, blasphemed as it is to-day, if every Christian were to do his duty here? But how is this duty carried out? There is not even a thought of discovering what the duty really is. There is hardly a single person, even in the most holy employments, who has ever seriously considered how far it is his duty to hallow the name of God, and there are still fewer who follow faithfully the light of their conscience. Are the words we recite no more then than an empty form? Do we think that we have discharged our whole duty by the mere recitation of the words?

You and I must always remember that when we say to God *Hallowed be thy name*, we must mean that his name is to be hallowed as much as it can be and as much as it ought to be by all those who are intended to hallow it, beginning with ourselves.

Do you understand all that is involved in this petition or desire?

The name of the true God is unknown to idolaters, who are found in great numbers in three-quarters of the world. You are praying that they may renounce their false deities and worship God only. You are praying him to enlighten those poor nations sitting in the shadow of death, praying him to send them zealous missionaries and bless their preaching, praying him to remove all obstacles set up by demons and the powers of the world against their conversion. If by any means whatsoever you have the opportunity of encouraging or forwarding this holy work, can you without any prick of conscience neglect it or use it carelessly? And if you should be in holy Orders and God should call you to take part in this great work, how could you be deaf to this call and not say like the prophet Isaiah: *Here am I, send me.*[1]

The religion of Jesus Christ, the only Son of God, is an abomination to the followers of Mahomet. You are asking God to open their eyes to the deception of this false prophet and to abolish finally this sect, which has triumphed for so many centuries in wide regions where Christianity once flour-

[1] Isa. 6: 8.

ished, and aspires to extend its sway until it has altogether destroyed our religion.

The Catholic Church, the centre of our religion, is slandered and persecuted by heretics and schismatics who have separated themselves from her with shameful violence, and have shut her up for three centuries within very narrow borders, this Church that should embrace the whole world. You are asking that they should acknowledge their errors, cast aside their unjust prejudices, renounce their obstinacy and fill the heart of their mother with joy by returning to her arms.

Licence and impiety threaten to invade all the domain that is still left to Christ and his Church. We have recently felt the effect of their effrontery in France, where they have unveiled their sinister designs, and had not a special Providence watched over the kingdom they would have executed these designs. Their zealous missionaries have spread the power of their detestable doctrines in the neighbouring countries, and the whole of Europe has seemed to be prepared as the scene of a general revolt against God and the Powers who represent him. You ask that this impious race, which does not even acknowledge the existence of a supreme Being and a natural law, should be converted or perish, and that the secular and ecclesiastical authorities should take the most righteous and effectual measures to nip the dangerous philosophy in the bud, and uproot it from every mind and heart.

In every place the various orders of the State have need of reform. The clergy need above all more knowledge and more holiness, since it is their duty to instruct and to show an example to everyone else. The terrible disasters that have lately almost destroyed the State and Church in France are a sufficient proof of this, and unless some speedy and lasting change should take place in our opinions and morals we shall inevitably have to face even greater sufferings. You ask in your prayer that all should look into their hearts, own their guilt, beg for divine mercy, and in the future repair by their blameless lives the evils and scandals they have caused. You ask in a word that every community, every family, every Christian should be holy with the holiness proper to their state of life, and that God should be glorified as he desires and as he ought to be glorified. The solemn prayers addressed to him by the Church on Good Friday are summed up in the simple words: *Hallowed be thy name.* Has that ever occurred to you? Are you beginning to understand how much is included in this short prayer?

Do you understand in particular the degree of perfection it demands of you? It demands that the chief desires of your heart, on which all other desires depend, should be the glory of the heavenly Father, and not only his glory but his greatest possible glory. It demands that you should work for it and yourself forward it in everything, every day and at every moment of the day. It demands that you should not be content with your efforts, but should ardently wish others to aim at the same end and surpass you. Finally, it demands that your zeal should exhaust and devour you, that you should live only for God and never cease to upbraid yourself for not glorifying him enough.

Is it so with us, with you who read these words and with me who write them?

Consider the intention of Jesus Christ in giving us this prayer and the meaning that he himself gave it. Consider the way in which he himself hallowed the Father's name, and that it was especially in this matter that he commanded us to imitate him. Consider what God is, what he desires, what he has done for you, what he has promised you, what he expects of you. Can a Christian possibly go too far when it is a question of glorifying him? It would indeed be blasphemy to think so. Once more I ask: how do we fulfil the object of this petition? It is the first and most important of all. We only deserve the name of Children of God in so far as we desire our Father's glory, and he will himself only glorify us to the extent that we have glorified him. What reward should we be justified in expecting from him if we were to die at this moment? Let us think it over quietly for it is worth our attention.

THY KINGDOM COME

In which kingdom do we wish God to reign?

This petition does not refer to the dominion that God exercises over nature as creator and preserver of all things, for the laws which he has established in that realm are always in force. No created being can frustrate them or escape them, and when by some miracle he interferes with them himself, it is always as an absolute Ruler that he acts by the use of his free sovereign will.

Nor does it refer to the reign of God's Providence in the moral world whereby he unfailingly causes his designs to be served by events, even those which depend on the free will of his creatures. The counsels of God are unchangeable; his decrees cannot fail to be carried out, and no man has the power to interfere with them, because all is foreseen and ordered accordingly.

Still less is it the dominion of justice and chastisement which God exercises, and will for ever exercise, over his rebellious creatures who have broken his commands. This dominion is in a sense involuntary, for it does not function by the immediate intention of God. It is we who by our obstinate disobedience force him to punish us, when he would rather be in a position to reward us. We cannot therefore desire for God a dominion that he does not desire for himself, being only forced to exercise it for our sins.

The kingdom for whose coming we pray is a dominion that is infinitely dear to him; it consists in the voluntary submission of man to his orders, the homage that man freely pays to him, recognizing that it is due to him on every consideration; and offering it with all love and loyalty. This supernatural dominion, source of God's glory and our own happiness, is free from all compulsion on his part. He commands, but we are free to obey or disobey; he suggests, entreats and urges by his grace, but it is in our power to resist; he reproaches us and fills us with keen remorse when we fail in our duty, but we can if we wish, disregard the reproaches and harden ourselves against the remorse. In short, we are left to decide for ourselves; we can choose to glorify God or offend him. Any other form of dominion over our wills would be contrary to his design and would bring no glory to him or merit to us. This is the dominion which is the object of the prayer taught us by Jesus Christ, and ought to be that of our most ardent desires. Nothing but love can give us those desires, of which the sincerity, force and efficacy will correspond to the degree of charity that is in our hearts.

This dominion of grace will only endure for the course of our mortal life and will be succeeded by an everlasting kingdom, in which God will reward our obedience and exercise his glory in making us happy. This second dominion is the end and aim of the first, and God will reign thus over us in his eternal kingdom only in so far as we have been submissive to the rule of his grace in this present life. It is our duty to desire the coming of these two kingdoms even more on God's account than our own, because his glory should be far more important to us than our own happiness.

But it is especially the first kingdom that we ought to desire, since that is the chief object of God's concern. This is the kingdom that brings him true honour and that he will never forget in the life to come when he will say to each one of his servants: Because I reigned over thee with all thy free consent, come and reign with me, and receive a reward according to the measure of the cost at which thou wast faithful to me to the end.

For we must have no illusions. God's temporal reign necessarily demands sacrifice from us and indeed, to speak truly, it demands a continual sacrifice; everything within and without

us is opposed to his dominion; everything prompts us to
shake off the yoke, and it is only through the ordeal of constant battles and struggles that we can persevere to the end.
There would be far less glory to God if we found less difficulty
in submission, and such a crown as is promised to us is indeed worth the longest labour and the most painful efforts.
After all, these labours and efforts are the result of the corruption of our nature and this corruption is the effect of sin
which was not willed but permitted by God. If Adam had
persevered in his state of innocence, and if we ourselves were
careful to maintain the condition of sanctifying grace which
was given us at our baptism, we should find the reign of God
in us easy and lightsome. The hardness and irksomeness we
must impute to ourselves. We must keep a stiff front against
the evil tendencies whence come all our obstacles, and thank
God for the abundant life he gives us to overcome them.

Every day we pray him to reign over us. But is it a prayer
that really comes from our hearts and do we do everything
that we can to promote his reign? Grace is the means that God
uses for the exercise of his rule. Are we submissive to grace?
Are we at all times attentive to listen to his teaching, and do we
obey it as soon as we understand it? Does God reign over our
senses, and do we permit nothing to them which is contrary
to his designs? Does he reign over our imagination, so that we
do not allow it to remove us from him by its distraction, or
lead us into harm? Does God reign over our passions, so that
we are careful to repress their first wrong impulses? Does he
reign over our mind, so that we strive to make our ideas conform to his and judge of things as he judges? He must reign
over our will. Do we not often resist his will, so that we are
full of impatience and revolt at the least contradiction? Do
we not rebel against the disposition of Providence when they
are not in line with our own plans, our own ideas, our own
inclinations?

Where is the soul over which God reigns absolutely and

without opposition? Where is the soul who laments his resistance to God's dominion, and humbles himself in a ceaseless prayer for a spirit of submission and docility, adding to his prayer all his efforts? They are rare enough, such Christians, not merely in the world where the devil has incomparably more servants than God, but even in the sanctuary and the cloister.

I do not for a moment mean that the opposition of truly devout persons to the reign of God is carried to the point of open rebellion; I am far from having such a bad and false opinion of them. There are still many Christians who would rather die than deliberately transgress one of God's commandments in any serious matter. But we cannot confine God's rule within these narrow limits. Can we profess to obey him from love when we are content to go no further than that? Surely God expects more of us than that. Would Jesus Christ have dictated to us a prayer that meant no more than this: that we could not resist orders given to us by his Father without incurring his displeasure? It is out of the question. Even an earthly father expects, and has a right to expect, more than that from his children. God, whose rights over us are infinitely greater, wishes to reign over us fully and perfectly. Jesus Christ understood that and wished us to understand it too. This perfect and total dominion embraces everything and leaves us no liberty to dispose of a single thought, word or deed. God by his grace must govern, rule and control the entire man at all times, in all places, in all circumstances. You cannot withhold anything from his sway; the very smallest exception would wound his jealousy.

Am I not then, you will ask, my own master in any way at all? No, you give up all rights over yourself every time you say: *Thy kingdom come;* if that is not your intention you are giving to the words an interpretation that God rejects. Remember, pray, that God's kingdom must necessarily share the infinity of his nature and cannot be compared with the reign of men whose rights are limited. God's rights have not and cannot have any limits, and if you set limits to them you detract from his dominion.

I cannot make too much of this point, because pride and self-love always tend to minimize our state of subjection.

Must not reason direct all your doings in virtue of your humanity, so that there is nothing in your actions of which reason cannot approve? What is this reason which imposes its law upon man in this way but the eternal reason? In like manner as you are a Christian, a creature with a supernatural destiny, you must in everything be directed by grace and keep your destiny in view in all your actions, which must therefore always be done from a supernatural motive. This cannot happen unless they are inspired by God and guided by a special movement on his part. Reason and grace then are the two means by which God exercises his dominion over you, and the two must work in harmony together if you are to be in subjection to him as a man and as a Christian. There is no question about this, and it is by this measure that you must estimate the extent of God's dominion over you and of your willing obedience to him.

Do not say to me: But I shall not be damned for some slight neglect of what is due to God, for who would be saved if one were forced to give him such an absolute dominion? I tell you plainly that any Christian who thinks after this fashion completely fails to enter into the spirit of the Lord's Prayer; he entirely misunderstands it. Remind yourself that in this prayer your own salvation is subordinated to the reign of God, which is the first object of it and far more important in itself than in its relation to you. There is no question of deciding how far you must allow God to reign in you in order to make certain your salvation. Who could define that exactly? No one in the world. Your own interests forbid you even to discuss the matter, for you would evidently be led astray.

Even supposing that it were possible to gauge the extent of

God's rule that was necessary for you, would it be fitting that a child of God should stop at that point? Surely a man would dishonour himself in the meanest way by limiting the rights of such a Father to his own necessities, considering only himself in his submission to him. You would be ashamed to show such feelings to an earthly father, and yet you act on these principles towards your Father who is in heaven without any shame. Ah! make sure that God is reigning in you and leave to him the care of your salvation. He is more able and willing to take care of it than you are, and he will be all the more ready to secure it, as he sees you more concerned with his interests than with your own. If you loved him and were able to give him even greater rights over you, ought you to hesitate for a moment? His fatherly authority is so gentle; no father ever used it so considerately. If his claims are so wide it is because he can demand no less without neglecting what is due to his honour; and, moreover, if the glory is his all the advantage here is yours. He cannot lose anything and you will gain everything.

Instead then of limiting the dominion of his grace over you, let it rather be your desire that his rule should extend to all mankind.

Add to the number of God's subjects.

See that he rules in your house and in every place where you have any authority. See that he rules over the souls that he has entrusted to your charge. Let your words, your examples, your good works, your preaching, your writing and all your enterprises aim always at winning hearts for him. Include the whole world in your intention when you say: *Thy Kingdom come.* Have a lively regard for everything that has to do with the honour of religion, the propagation of the faith and the advance of piety. If you must work yourself to death, endure every sort of cruel trial and shed your blood in this glorious cause, count yourself fortunate, for fortunate you would indeed be.

Such should be the desire of every Christian.

The Lord's Prayer is intended to arouse such desires, to maintain them and strengthen them in the Christian's heart every day.

May it from this moment so work in your heart.

THY WILL BE DONE, IN EARTH AS IT IS IN HEAVEN

What a perfect aspiration that is!

We pray that God shall find no more opposition to his will than he finds in the Blessed Ones.

It is impossible to wish or to ask for anything more perfect than this, and if we obtained our wish and practised what we prayed for God would be obeyed as promptly, as lovingly, as disinterestedly, by his children on earth as by the angels and saints in heaven. Only one will prevails in heaven, *God's will*. There it has complete dominion always, in every way and over everything, and there is no obstacle in the way of it. We can say even more: everything works together towards that dominion, and no desire can exist except for its complete fulfilment. Why is not Heaven earth's model? Why are we not in this matter the faithful image of the saints in glory? It is our heavenly Father's will, it is Christ's intention, and it was for that purpose that he taught us the Lord's Prayer.

No desire is more natural for children, no request is more reasonable. The man in whose heart the desire is not found is not honouring God as he deserves, and is not worthy to call him by the name of Father. For he is no more the God of Heaven than of earth; he is no more the Father of the Blessed than he is yours. He has the same claims on our obedience, therefore, as on theirs and his will, the origin of order, is essentially the only law of every intelligent creature, whether still upon the road, or come to the end of the journey.

If we are endowed with free will it is to give value to our submission, which would otherwise possess none; it is not that we may be free to follow our own will. Liberty does not give us the right to dispose of ourselves and repudiate God's dominion over us. How could we glorify him and make ourselves worthy of an eternal reward if we were not free? It was for these two ends that God created us free and not by any means to dispense us from giving him his due. The imperfection of liberty in the world consists in the possibility of our abusing it by preferring our own will to God's. In Heaven, as St. Augustine shows, this defect in liberty will be removed; it will no longer be possible to make a bad use of it, and it will be entirely directed to the willing of God's will. "It is not true," says the holy doctor, "that the Blessed will have no free will because sin will no longer attract them; on the contrary they will be all the more free since they will be freed from taking pleasure in sinning, so that they are unable to feel any pleasure except that of not sinning. For (he adds) the free will that was given to man at the beginning, in his original state of rectitude at his creation, was so entirely capable of not sinning that it was also capable of sinning; whereas in this final state his free will will be all the stronger because it will be incapable of sinning."[1] In that respect it will approach the divine liberty, the perfection of which consists in absolute incapacity for sin.

Our present liberty, therefore, which is a gift from God, does not absolve us from making his will our law as it is the law of the Saints in Heaven, and what makes their condition infinitely preferable to ours is that they no longer possess the disastrous power to disobey the law, the power that creates all the disorder and danger in our condition. In the Lord's Prayer we ask that this power remains unexercised, that we may never use it to oppose the divine will in the very least. No doubt we must fight, and fight strenuously and without intermission, to attain this end. What however makes this strife necessary is not our liberty but our evil tendencies, which have nothing in common with liberty and are the result of our natural imperfection so much increased by sin.

[1] De civit. Dei xxii, c. 30.

I

The reason why the divine will meets with no resistance in Heaven is that no created object entices the created being to oppose it, for there is no appeal to the senses, imagination or passions, since some of these have ceased to exist and the others are satisfied with the possession of the Supreme Good. There is no longer any individual mind or will or personal interest. Things are seen and judged as God sees and judges them. Since there is no way of thinking other than his, he is opposed in nothing; what he approves is approved by all, what he condemns is condemned by all. Moreover the created will as it exists in Heaven has no desire, affection or determination that it can call its own, the fruit of its own being; it loves all that God loves because he loves it, and hates all that God hates because he hates it. As for self-love and self-seeking, all that is entirely banished from Heaven. No interests are acknowledged there but God's interests, no love is known but the love of God; even individual bliss is valued only in subordination to God's good pleasure or rather the bliss of the individual is so intense in itself that it derives no value from personal possession. There is then no motive for any wish apart from God's will, nor for wishing anything otherwise than as he wishes it.

Such is the state of perfection at which the Christian must aim on earth, and it is to this end that the Gospel so expressly commands him to detach himself from created objects and to renounce self. Why this detachment? Because external objects attract him, so that, seduced by their deceptive claims, he inclines to yield to them against the will of God, who commands him to love him alone and everything else only in relation to him. Why this renunciation of self? Because pride is a cause of independence, and self-love is an exclusive love which makes a man use everything in relation to himself and make his personal interests the cause of every action. So he is led to direct a constant opposition to the will of God, who cannot allow his creatures to aspire to independence or focus their affections on themselves. Unless the Christian strives with all his might to put himself in the same disposition as the Blessed, he will never be disposed to fulfil the divine will as it is done in Heaven, and yet he is commanded to pray every day that he as well as others may do so.

To say that God encounters no obstacle to his will in Heaven matters little; his will is fulfilled at the first sign with love and joy, and to carry it out is an honour and delight for which everything may be sacrificed.

St. Francis de Sales says in so many words that "the saints in Heaven are in such close union with the will of God that if there were a little more of his good pleasure to be done in hell they would leave Paradise to go there."[1] He expresses himself no less forcibly in several passages of the *Treatise on the Love of God*. It is useless to object that the supposition is impossible. We are well aware of that, but that is not the question. The question is the inmost disposition of the saints in Heaven and that must be such as has just been said. The reason is that they see nothing, not merely preferable, but comparable, to the will of God, and in their minds his good pleasure is beyond everything without a single exception. Were this not so their charity would be neither pure nor well-regulated; they would love God otherwise than as he loves himself and they would love themselves as much as, or more than, God, which would be inconsistent with the heavenly state and condition.

This is the model which Jesus Christ puts before us, and he could not give us one that was less perfect without infringing his Father's rights. The Christian must aspire to accomplish everything that God wills, however hard it may be, the moment it is known to him, without delay, without hesitation and without yielding to any repugnance he may feel; to accomplish it with love, with devotion to this will for its own sake as seen to be above everything else, and giving to this motive such a pre-eminence over all other motives that it is sufficient

Entretien II: De la Confiance.

in itself to make him carry it out joyfully and proudly, as though there were no other kind of happiness, as indeed there is not.

But does Jesus Christ really mean that there is no difference here between the inhabitants of Heaven and those of earth?

Yes, he means that there is no difference as far as the ground and disposition of the will are concerned. This must be so, since God is as much our God as the God of the Blessed and his good pleasure no less our supreme good than theirs. Where then does the difference lie? For there must be a difference, a very great difference. It consists in this: that there are obstacles in the way of our submission whereas the Blessed have none to overcome, that we have feelings of repugnance from which they are free, that we are liable to fail more or less in fulfilling God's will, while they have nothing of the kind to fear. Besides our obedience is a merit on account of its difficulties and theirs is a reward. It is because they have fought that they need fight no more, it is because they have overcome their feelings of repugnance that they have them no more, it is because they have been faithful unto death that they are certain of being faithful always. These differences, it will be seen, are matters of condition and not of feeling or disposition which ought to be the same in them and in ourselves. It must needs cost us something to do God's will here on earth, in order that we may have no difficulty in submitting to it in heaven. But the suffering we endure now, that comes from the corruption of our nature, ought not to weaken the determination of our will; on the contrary that determination should be all the stronger and more courageous on that account.

Is it possible, you ask me, that God's will should be done on earth as perfectly as it is done in Heaven? Is not this a mere wish, an ideal to which human weakness cannot attain?

If the thing were not possible would Jesus Christ have made it one of the chief petitions of his prayer? Without doubt he knew our weakness better than we, but he also knew the power of grace and what it can accomplish in a heart entirely given up to it. Here we must apply the words that he used in another context: *With men this is impossible but with God all things are possible.*[1] Man left to himself can do nothing, but upheld by grace he can do all things, as St. Paul was not afraid to say. With the help of grace it is possible to have a sincere desire to carry out the divine will as it is done by the saints in Heaven. It is possible after much resistance, hesitation and murmurings, to become humble and repentant for everything, to resolve to fall into such sin no more and finally to arrive at entire conformity with the will of God. Human frailty, great as we know it to be, is capable of this perfection; the saints are the proof of that. Nevertheless for all their sanctity they were not able to avoid some trivial faults. But their momentary errors into which they were surprised did not affect their permanent disposition, or make them less dependent on the good pleasure of God.

Now this is precisely what God requires of us, what Jesus Christ bids us pray for and what ought to be the aim of the Christian life.

Let us examine our own life in this light.

Every day I say to God: *They will be done in earth as it is in heaven.* Do I carry out his will in everything that depends on myself, and submit to it in all that does not depend on me? This thought: *God wills it*, is it the ruling motive in all my actions? Is it my support and consolation in all that I have to suffer? Do I strive to conform myself more and more to the divine will, obliging the foolish reasoning of my mind and the rebellions of my heart to yield to it? Is it my notion of a perfect life that I should co-operate with Providence, forming no projects of my own, disposing of myself in no way whatsoever, content with all that happens to me.

If after careful examination you can be sure that this is your habitual state of mind, then your repetition of the Lord's

[1] Matt. 19: 26.

Prayer is bearing fruit, and you are fulfilling the intention of the God-Man who taught it to you. If you cannot give this assurance, you are mistaken in supposing that you possess the spirit of the Christian faith and its divine Author.

For the rest, no one expects you all at once to reach the highest point of perfection. Who does not know that the Christian life is a continual apprenticeship and that there is always something to learn, however advanced one may be?

Do not be alarmed then by the ideal of perfection that is put before you and do not make it a reason for declining the undertaking. What is asked of you is a firm determination to submit yourself in everything to God's will, unceasing persistence in practising that submission even if the struggle costs you pain sometimes, a sincere repentance each time that you fail in it and a prompt and faithful return to it at the first warning of grace. This is the plan on which you ought to regulate your conduct, the plan which you ought to wish, advise and inspire others to adopt, encouraging them at need by word and example and helping them with your prayers.

If you reject all this as involving a perfection too exalted, if you think that God's will is limited to his express orders, accompanied by terrible threats, then you are degrading the name of a Child of God, weakening in yourself the spirit of adoption, and showing that you have not the least conception of the obedience due to such a Father.

Let us linger a moment on these three first petitions once more and dwell on the most important thought which is this: They were the foundation of the prayer of Jesus Christ during his earthly life.

What did he say to his Father in his prayers? Nothing but this: *Hallowed be thy name! Thy kingdom come! Thy will be done in earth as it is in heaven!* God and Man as he was he could neither form a holier prayer nor have in his heart desires more pure; his whole life was a perfect fulfilment of them. Forgetting himself he cared for nothing but the sanctification of his Father's name; he thought about nothing but the establishment of his Father's kingdom; he had no other sustenance than his Father's will; to it he dedicated himself when he entered the world, and when he left the world he sacrificed himself that it might be fulfilled. Immediately before his Passion he said to himself: I have glorified thee on the earth: I have finished the work which thou gavest me to do. . . . I have manifested thy name unto the men which thou gavest me out of the world.

According to these three titles which are really comprehended in one, as Son of God by nature speaking to his brothers by adoption, as Master teaching his disciples, as Chief of the elect revealing the road to heaven to the members of his mystical body, he should not, neither could he, have given us any other prayer relating to God than the prayer he offered himself. How glorious that Jesus Christ has condescended to associate me with his prayer! But also what shame if I do not repeat it with the same sentiments as he did, if I excuse myself for not having these sentiments on the ground that they are too perfect, if I should be so wicked and insane as to regard my little mind and heart as the measure of what I owe to the hallowing of God's name, the spreading of God's kingdom and the fulfilment of God's will! I had never understood till now all the beauty, sublimity and perfection of the Christian doctrine, the full extent of the duties it enjoins. But now I am well instructed and fully persuaded. I see that I have not even begun to be a Christian. It is high time for me to adopt the mind of Jesus Christ and imitate his conduct, since I pray the prayer that was his.

GIVE US THIS DAY OUR DAILY BREAD

There is not a single word in this petition that does not contain useful lessons.

The first is that it is God who like the father of a family feeds all his children. To deserve their food they must earn it by labour and industry. This is the general law laid down at the time of the first sin. God said to Adam: *In the sweat of thy brow shalt thou eat bread*. The earth which originally produced everything naturally now only yields her fruit to a laborious cultivation. This is the penance imposed by God on sinful man; it is only on these terms that he consents to supply him with bread.

But he further desires man to recognize that he derives his bread from God's goodness and to ask him for it, for in truth man's labour would be unrewarded and fruitless unless God blessed it.

It is not man who endows the earth with inexhaustible fertility, it is not he who gives the seed its power of multiplying, it is not he who develops the plant by rain coupled with the heat of the sun, and brings it by degrees to complete maturity.

Agriculture is the most important but it is not the only work to which God has subjected man. Every occupation of mind or body, necessary or useful for the support of human society, is included in the sentence pronounced against the first man and no man who does not work in some way or other, or works in a way that is useless or harmful, deserves the bread he eats or has any right to ask for it. If God gives it to him it is only by way of his general Providence by which *he maketh his sun to rise on the evil and on the good and sendeth rain on the just and on the unjust*.[1]

So our prayer to him for food and the other necessaries of life by no means dispenses us from labour, rather it implies work since work is a title to food; moreover God supplies our food in such a way that our care and toil are needed to gather and preserve it, or to prepare it and adapt it for our use. Nor do our labours dispense us from the gratitude we owe to God, author of all our blessings.

This petition manifestly condemns every method of gain that is wrong or harmful to others, for God could not be re-

[1] Matt. 5: 45.

garded as the source of benefits that were wrongfully obtained. How could anyone have the effrontery to say to him: Give us our bread, when in order to get it he employs fraud and violence against God's express command? That is not asking for it but snatching it from him against his wish. So any man whose conscience reproaches him for using unlawful means to acquire temporal goods is unworthy to repeat the Lord's Prayer, and should he do so is pronouncing his own condemnation.

Give us

It is not only for yourself and your family that you ask for bread, but for all your brother Christians and indeed for all mankind. You ought to be as much concerned about their food as your own, since you are all children of the same Father. It is culpable avarice on your part then to wish to possess more than others, it is insane pride to fancy that you deserve more, it is flagrant injustice to diminish or perhaps even appropriate their share in order to increase your own, just as it is mean jealousy that makes you envy your neighbour when God gives more to him than to you. When you say: Give us, you let God be distributor and do not expect to make him apportion the shares exactly as you wish.

On the other hand, if God has given you much and your neighbour is without the necessaries of life, you are obliged in virtue of this prayer to share your goods with him and to use your abundance for the relief of his need. For God desires to give to everybody, he bids you pray for all men and he does not understand this prayer, Give us, in a sense restricted to your personal needs. If then he should give you more than you need and leave your brother in want, it is not because he forgets him, it is because he wishes to give to him by your hands, to make both of you practise the virtues of your station and bring you together by compassionate generosity on the one hand and gratitude on the other. Therefore, when your

brother asks you in God's name for his share which happens
to be in your possession and you refuse him, you are not only
being cruel and inhuman, but you are keeping something
which is not your own, but placed in your hands as a trustee
and given to you only that you may pass it on to the needy.

Give us this day

It is for to-day that you ask provision and not for to-
morrow. The morrow, when it comes, will take thought for
itself, says Jesus Christ. You are alive to-day and need bread
for to-day, and God, who has pledged himself to provide for
your real needs, is ready to give it you. But you do not know if
you will be alive to-morrow. It is then a foresight that is not
only useless but disturbing, to think to-day of to-morrow's
bread, and God, who desires you to rely day by day on his
Providence, does not approve of your worrying about your
necessary supplies in advance. Consider how a child regards
his father and mother in relation to his needs. Most of the
time he thinks of them not at all. Food, clothing, all his necessaries are provided for him without his asking; his parents'
love sees to everything. If he should happen to ask, it is only
for the needs of the moment; it is not in his nature to hoard,
to make any provision for the future. Such a thing would
show a lack of trust which could not fail to displease his
parents and chill their affection. Have you forgotten what
Jesus Christ more than once repeats: that children are your
pattern and that the Kingdom of Heaven is for those who are
like them? Do not worry your Father by mistrusting him, do
not worry about the day that is to come; he has thought of it
for you, he has foreseen everything and made all the necessary
arrangements.

Avarice which has never enough and amasses wealth to
provide, not for days and months, but for years and centuries,
is of course condemned by this petition, even when this hoard-
ing does no one any harm.

Detachment from temporal blessings is also prescribed. For what greater detachment is there than limiting our claim on possessions to the present moment, so that possession becomes merely a temporary use? Complete trust in Providence is enjoined, not in the sense that Jesus Christ forbids a certain amount of foresight, but that he condemns over-anxious caution, over-eager cares and the habit of making worries for ourselves to save us from worries that may never arise. Is he not right? Is not this a great benefit to us? Can we deny that the thought, *What shall I live on to-morrow?* poisons the life of to-day, and that most men are far more depressed by their fears for the future than by their discomforts in the present? I have earned my bread hitherto, says the artisan, but who will give it to me in my old age? My business is doing very well, says the merchant, but it may not always be so, and if it should come to grief what would become of me? I have a large family, says one man, and for the moment I am in a position to support it; but when my children are grown up and I have to settle them, where shall I find the means and what shall I have left for myself? My health, says another, is all that I and my wife and children have to depend on; supposing I were to fall ill or become infirm how should I support them; if I should die while they are young what will become of them? How mad they are! Why give way to such fruitless thoughts which only distress you and wear you out? Eat with a quiet mind the bread God gives you to-day, and for the morrow trust in his fatherly goodness. These cares which wear you out, and are as harmful to your soul as to your body, will not preserve you from the accidents you fear and foresee in the distant future. Only God can save you from them, and what other means have you for persuading him to do so than by putting your trust in him?

Give us our bread

Note well that what you are asking for is bread, what is necessary for life. When God has given that to you he has fulfilled his promise, and you have no cause for complaint against him. He owes you nothing you may desire beyond that.

You may say that necessities cannot be understood too strictly and there must be a certain latitude. I agree, but is it for you or for God to determine how much? If it is you who make the decision, you will not believe that you have what is necessary for your position; as long as a single person richer than you could be found in your position, you would always think yourself poor in proportion to his advantage over you. Do not consult then your own avarice nor your ambitious views nor the maxims of the world, which finds its happiness in wealth. If what you have is really enough do not desire more; do not regret what you have lost, if you can do without it; be sure that in the eyes of the wise, and still more for the Christian, a modest competence is better than riches for securing peace in this life and happiness in the life to come.

Our daily bread

You ask every day because every day your need is renewed.

God, in his goodness towards you, wishes to keep you continuously dependent in body as well as in soul. It is generally seen that those who live by the daily earnings of manual labour or by their own industry think more of God and his Providence, are more concerned to appeal to him, more ready to thank him and more full of trust in him, than the rich whose wealth is assured to them, and who do not look to God for daily benefits. Far too often they forget him and only remember their need of him when they suffer, or are on the point of suffering, some serious loss. Then they turn to him again, begging him to give them success in their affairs. No doubt this is something, but what a difference there is between this forced return to God and the constant return of the Christian, who comes to receive his daily bread from him. What a difference in this respect between the rich man who is never

afraid of being in want, and the poor man who looks to Heaven
for the alms without which he could not live, for whom a
morsel of bread and the smallest coin is a gift of Providence.

But since the Lord's Prayer is meant for us all, let us, rich
and poor, share in Christ's intention when we make this petition, reminding ourselves that those who are abundantly supplied with temporal blessings have just as many virtues to
practise as those who have few possessions or none. Let us
remember above all that spiritual needs must take precedence
of temporal, and that to relieve the body even when its necessity is most pressing we must never risk our soul's salvation.
There are many who think that the pressure of their necessities excuses the sins they commit. They are deluded and their
conscience plays them false. The true Christian never com-
promises his eternal interests, never allows himself even to
think that the necessities of life authorize him to offend God.
Rather than be guilty of such an error he will beg his bread if
he can do nothing else, submitting to the humiliation, if not
with joy, at least with resignation. After the appalling disaster
that has ruined so many families in our country, the lesson is
very appropriate and everyone should remember it whatever
his position may be, whenever he repeats the *Paternoster*.
What a reversal of all order if a Christian who should not ask
anything for himself, should begin by praying for the hallowing of his Father's name, the coming of his kingdom and the
perfect fulfilment of his will, and then should not only think
of his own interests before God's but also, in order to preserve his life and save himself from temporal need, should
consider it a small matter to displease the best of Fathers.

FORGIVE US OUR DEBTS AS WE FORGIVE OUR DEBTORS

In several passages the Gospel represents our sins as a debt
that we have contracted towards God's justice, and the pardon granted to us as a remission of that debt. That is why, in
order to make the matter clearer and more intelligible, the

words of Jesus Christ have been translated in our language
into those which have the same sense: *Forgive us our trespasses
as we forgive them that trespass against us.*

The conditional petition is very remarkable. Nothing shows
more clearly how important the forgiveness of injuries seems
to God. He here solemnly pledges himself to remit the sins we
have committed against him, if we on our side will forgive our
neighbour for the wrong he has done to us. But at the same
time he declares that we may expect no pardon from him if we
are adamant towards our brothers. And in order, as it were,
to force us to forgive, he bids us use a form of prayer in which
we definitely engage to do it. *Forgive us,* we say to him, *as we
forgive;* which is as much as to say: *Forgive us if we forgive and
do not forgive us if we refuse to forgive.*

The vindictive Christian is then condemned here out of his
own mouth; or else he must cease to say the Lord's Prayer as
long as any thought of vengeance remains in his heart. It is a
dreadful alternative for anyone who has any religious belief
at all. Jesus Christ foresaw how much the forgiveness of injuries would cost our pride and self-love, and how we should
cast about for reasons for avoiding it; it is therefore in order
to cut short this debate, to impose silence and overcome our
pride and self-love, that he appeals to our strongest interest,
making the forgiveness of injuries the essential condition of
the far more important forgiveness that we need ourselves,
and pray God every day to give us. Moreover of all the petitions that make up this prayer this is the only one on which he
enlarges and insists, adding immediately these words: *For if ye
forgive men their trespasses, your heavenly Father will also forgive you. But if ye forgive not men their trespasses, neither will
your Father forgive your trespasses.*[1]

Which of us has not offended God? Which of us does not
ask forgiveness of his sins? Which of us is not more or less
uneasy about that forgiveness and does not long for some as-

[1] Matt. 6: 14, 15.

surance that may bring him peace? Well, here is a definite assurance and it is Jesus Christ who gives it you. If your brother has offended you and you are seriously disposed to forgive him; if you feel no hatred and resentment against him; if on the first advance he makes or the first sign of regret he shows, you are gladly reconciled to him; if in certain cases you go ahead of him and make the first advances; finally, if you are resolved to forgive him in the same way as many times as he offends you, then you may be at ease and fully confident about the forgiveness of your own sins. You have every reason to believe that it will be given to you and you are allowed to say to God: *Lord, I am guilty in thy sight and I deserve no mercy, but I have forgiven my brother from my heart as thou hast commanded me; I hope, yes indeed, I hope all things from thy compassion and I found my hope on thy promises which cannot fail.* Is there for a Christian, who understands what happiness he loses through sin and to what retribution sin exposes him, any consolation to compare with this?

On the other hand, what desolation, what despair, what bitter assurance of eternal retribution, if he obstinately refuses to pardon, and if he maintains in his heart right up to his last breath sentiments of vengeance. His sentence is passed and he has signed his own condemnation. It has been put out of his power to say to God: *Forgive me,* and having shown no mercy to his neighbour he can only expect a merciless judgment. He knows it, for there is no truth more clearly and frequently expressed in the Gospel, and the *Paternoster* which he has repeated since childhood bears witness against him.

Suppose he takes it on himself, as some have done, to suppress or change this petition. Is he the Master? What will he gain? Will Jesus Christ authorize the suppression or the change? Will it not rather be an added sin?

How dreadful is the state of a heart dedicated to hatred! It is premature damnation. Nevertheless it is not a rare state, and human pride is insane enough to undertake its justification. The man of vindictive heart dares to complain that God has imposed too hard a condition on him and charges God with injustice. Wretched creature, you owe your master ten thousand talents and he has pity on you and remits your debt; a moment later you seize your brother by the throat because he owes you a hundred pence. You strangle him, crying: *Pay me that thou owest*. You pay no attention to his apologies and entreaties, and you think it unjust that God should treat you as you treat your fellow-men. Man refuses forgiveness to his fellow-man for offences that are slight, since they are between equals, and at the same time expects God to forgive him for offences against his infinite Majesty. What unbounded pride and injustice!

Is it not clear that God in this matter concedes a portion of his rights, and that he could not offer us more favourable terms? The debts that we have incurred by sinning against him cannot possibly be compared with those that men incur amongst themselves by their mutual offences. God on the one hand is prepared to remit all our debts at our first request, and demands on the other hand that charity and peace shall reign among us, because it is his design to unite us eternally in his own bosom where charity and peace abide. Could he possibly then demand less of us to reconcile us with himself, than perfect reconciliation with our brothers? Jesus Christ, in whose mind our sins were present on the cross, and who shed his blood for us, though it was we who crucified him no less than the Jews, is surely not asking too much when he expects us to forgive one another as he has forgiven. Nothing appears more just to our arrogant reason than vengeance; according to the principles of Christianity nothing is more unjust. Even if we were guiltless of any offence towards God, the example of Jesus Christ would impose upon us the obligation to forgive and we should be guilty for not having followed it.

LEAD US NOT INTO TEMPTATION

What are we asking of God in these words?

It is impossible that he should tempt us himself or put us in any position approaching offence to him. God tests but he does not tempt, that is to say, does not invite or drive anyone to evil. It is one thing to train virtue by trials and quite another thing to awaken and incite in a man his evil tendencies. *God cannot be tempted with evil*, says St. James, *neither tempteth he any man: but every man is tempted when he is drawn away by his own lust and enticed.*[1] And it is not God who endowed man with concupiscence: it is the work of sin and has its sources in the radical imperfection of our nature. This is what tempts us from within. From without, the devil, by the permission of God who desires our spiritual good, works on our imagination, rouses our passions, labours to corrupt our minds by false reasoning and to seduce our will by alluring suggestions. His aim is to involve us in his ruin and to injure, as far as he can, God's glory. This is why he is called by the Scripture the *Tempter*. But God leads no one into temptation, except in the same sense as he hardens *by withdrawing his help*, as St. Augustine says, when a man has made himself unworthy of it, *and not by communicating malice to him*.

Nor do we ask him not to allow us to be tempted. Adam was tempted in his state of innocence: God allowed it for good reasons although he foresaw his fall, and after the first sin man became still more subject to temptations than he was before. Moreover they are the test of our faithfulness; they are necessary to keep us humble and rouse us to vigilance and prayer. They can only hurt us as far as we wish. Grace to resist them never fails us except by our own fault. They can be helpful to us in producing deeds of singular virtue and in acquiring merits, and we need them to teach us not only how to meet them fearlessly but how to fight and conquer

[1] Jas., 1: 13 14.

K

them. Incarnate God himself allowed the evil one to tempt him.

What we ask in this petition then is that God will not permit us to yield to temptation; that he will temper it to our strength, that he will come to our help, protecting us by his grace from the snares and assaults of the devil, and will fortify our will against the lures of concupiscence. We say this prayer every day because there is not a single day, or indeed a single moment, in which we are not or may not be in danger of sinning. Sin has made its home in our heart, and the roaring lion ceaselessly circles round us seeking an opportunity to surprise and devour us. Every age and every condition of life has its own temptations; neither a holy vocation, nor retirement from the world, nor even solitude, can free us from temptation and the most subtle and dangerous attacks of all threaten those who have advanced furthest in the way of perfection, unless they are extremely watchful.

Therefore, of all the petitions of the Lord's Prayer this is in a sense the most necessary, since right up to our latest breath we live on the verge of the abyss, always on the point of falling into it and it is death alone that can establish us in that state of peace, from which at any moment of our life we may fall.

Enclosed in this petition is a double confession: first, we confess the corruption of our nature, a corruption deeper than we can imagine and only to be known by the precautions necessary to save us from it; secondly, we confess our frailty which is extreme, permitting us to count neither on our dispositions nor our good habits nor our firmest resolutions. A trivial temptation, an indiscreet glance, a fugitive thought, a desire that seems to pass over the soul like a light breath, are all that is needed to defeat us and ruin us beyond recall. Even after we have long resisted a temptation so that we imagine ourselves to be free of it, if then we congratulate ourselves ever so little on that long resistance instead of attributing it entirely to grace, if then we should become less vigilant, less constant and fervent in prayer, it will return and attack us with greater violence and will overcome us. A thousand fatal examples are proof of this and we should become wise from the experience of others.

Every time then that we repeat the *Paternoster* let us recall our own miserable weakness, let us glance at the dangers that surround us and the foes that threaten us from every quarter; let us acknowledge our continual need of grace, humbly recognizing that if with grace we can do all things, without it we can do nothing. Let us not cease to ask God to give it to us and let us not of our rashness and presumption make ourselves unworthy to receive it.

God owes it to us in virtue of his promises, and he never refuses it when our temptation has come to us in a setting ordained by Providence, and when foreseeing the danger we confidently appeal to him, or when again we have been taken unawares by pitfalls that we could not possibly have foreseen. He owes it, and never refuses it, to the man who always mistrusts himself, who, having a deep conviction of his own weakness takes in good time all the measures suggested by Christian prudence. He owes it, and never refuses it, to the man who is faithful in small things in order to attain to faithfulness in things that are great.

The grace that God grants us at such times is not simply one of the ordinary gifts of grace, which suffice to justify his Providence and preserve it from all reproach, but which do not keep us from sinning; it is a special grace which supports us wonderfully and always produces the effect for which it is needed. Such graces as this are reserved by God for those souls who have made every effort to gain them. Observe that I am speaking only of habitual graces, and not of those prevenient graces by which God sometimes attracts the greatest sinners to himself. The foolhardy man who goes out rashly to meet dangers without consulting God's will; the presumptuous man who relies on his own strength, his acquired virtues, his past victories or the notions of a passing fervour; the slothful and luke-warm who neglect the small sins that are called trivial, because of themselves they do not deal death to the soul; these must not count on the divine assurance in great temptations, or in circumstances of special difficulty. These men have run into dangers through their own fault, they have presumed on their own strength, they have weakened themselves by a long series of small infidelities, they are fated to fall deplorably and perhaps will never recover themselves. So let us remember when we ask God to keep us from being overcome by temptation, that the petition applies only to those temptations which he himself has permitted and for which our habitual fidelity has prepared us and, so to speak, armed us; or, at the most, to those temptations into which we have been led by good intentions, imprudence, thoughtlessness, lack of vigilance, indiscreet zeal or an ill-timed desire to please.

God, who sees the inmost depths of the heart, does not forsake any sincere and earnest soul, and if he allows it to fall it is only that thus it may become more humble and more watchful.

We cannot fail to see that the world, I mean the world which still keeps up some appearance of Christianity, is full of snares. Everything in it tends to corrupt the mind by false maxims, which more or less distort the Gospel's holy severity, and to corrupt the heart by luring it into sensuality, avarice, or ambition. To love the world, to seek the world's approval, to fear its censure, its sneers and mockery, is clearly to run the risk of being overcome by the various temptations that meet us at every turn. It would be a gross mistake to hope for grace to preserve us from trials into which we had light-heartedly flung ourselves.

But also we must not be faint-hearted, and we must not doubt that help comes to us from above in all the outward temptations that inevitably arise from the state of life in which God has placed us, and from the duties that are laid upon us

by zeal and charity, as well as in the inward temptations that
are involved in the practice of the Christian virtues. We must
be ready to withstand fierce assaults of the devil, if we are resolved to devote ourselves entirely to God. But at the same
time we must not question for a moment the reality of the
divine protection, or doubt that it will give us victory over the
spirit of darkness.

We must never imitate those who in their fear of perdition
shun every opportunity of striving to save souls, lest they
should be led into offending God; nor those who renounce
the spiritual life because of their dread of the traps laid by the
devil along the path, and the cruel temptations that must
sometimes be faced. This is to insult the goodness and almighty love of our heavenly Father; it is to believe that the
devil, who only acts by the permission of God and cannot
overstep the limits that God has set to his power, can do more
to harm us than God can do to protect us; it is to renounce all
efforts to glorify God, to sanctify ourselves, and to work for
the sanctification of our neighbours. Let us go forward with
confidence between the two perils of presumption and faint-
heartedness, and we shall never ask God in vain to stand by
us in the hour of temptation.

BUT DELIVER US FROM EVIL. AMEN

Nothing is more important for us than to understand exactly
what is the evil from which Jesus Christ teaches us to pray for
deliverance. For in everything, and more especially here, his
ideas are the only guide of ours and all depends on our con-
forming to them closely. As the supreme good for the rational
creature is the eternal enjoyment of God's presence for which
he is destined, so his supreme evil is to be for ever deprived of
that presence. This is what his condemnation and damnation
mean. Deliverance from this great disaster is then the chief
object of our last petition. By faith only can we form any conception of the evil of being deprived of the enjoyment of

God's presence by our own fault, and indeed even the strongest faith can only give us a most imperfect idea of it in this world. Our weakness cannot support its full comprehension, which would make upon us such a strong impression as would cripple the freedom of our actions.

No amount of thinking can enable us to imagine the state of the soul at the moment of separation from the body, when she sees and feels that God is lost to her beyond recall. She knows then, with a clear and distinct knowledge, what God is in himself, what he is in relation to her, the infinite loss she has suffered and the impossibility of repairing it. The other objects that attracted her and occupied her in her life mean nothing to her now, she can no longer care for them or love them because she sees clearly their nothingness. Besides, death has robbed her of them all and if she thinks of them still, it is only to bemoan her intense folly in having attached herself to them. The desire of happiness is as strong and constant as ever, a desire as keen as it is inexpressible, a desire which will never have fulfilment; it will never be diverted nor deceived by any false enjoyment. Of that the soul is certain and all hope must be abandoned for ever. I say it again: the pain is inexpressible, both in its nature and in its continuity and duration. No condition of man on this earth, however terrible, however long, however desperate one may imagine it to be, can give us the least idea of this torment, because no earthly condition resembles the total loss of God.

This then is the evil from which the Christian prays to be delivered beyond all others, the evil that he must fear supremely and make every effort to avoid. To avoid it he need only preserve himself from another evil, by which alone he can be led into the first.

This second evil is sin, for which damnation is the just punishment. The one is the cause and the other is the effect, the inevitable consequence, as long as the cause is not removed. Jesus Christ's intention then is that the Christian should ask God with ever greater fervour to deliver him from sin, either by keeping him from falling into it, or by putting forth a hand to raise him as quickly as possible, lest he should die in that fatal state. At our first mortal sin God can cut the thread of our lives and cast us into hell; he can let us heap crime upon crime and with perfect justice refuse us any special grace, without which we can never recover divine love. As nothing can make us sure that he will not do what he can do, we are always to live in fear of offending him mortally.

But although the kind of sin which deals death to the soul is the chiefest evil, all sin is an evil, because it wounds the soul and makes it sick, weak and languid. A trivial fault leads to one that is more serious, and if we are not careful to avoid the smallest faults we are in the way of committing grave sin, and all the more so because there is no general rule that can determine the matter. It is not then enough, if we are to fulfil the intention of Jesus Christ, to pray to God to deliver us from mortal sin; every Christian should pray to be preserved from committing any sin deliberately and consciously.

Moreover, if he truly loves God, he will make the request, rather in order to avoid offending such a good Father, than from fear of falling a victim of divine vengeance. For sin is an evil, it is even God's only evil; not because it harms him but because it displeases him mightily and is the object of his hatred.

Therefore, since the Christian ought to love God rather than himself, it is right that he should have a greater horror of sin because it is an evil to God, than because it is injurious to himself.

Here is the true meaning of those words of the Lord's Prayer: *But deliver us from evil.*

These are the words of faith, and faith knows no evils but supernatural evils which wound God's holiness and stain the soul's purity, depriving it of sanctifying grace, or putting it in danger of losing it and so exposing it to eternal loss.

Are these our thoughts, these the deepest feelings of our hearts when we say this prayer?

Can the Christian, who knows himself to be living in mortal sin and actually deserves to be sent to hell, pray to God sincerely to deliver him from evil, when he is doing nothing for his part to respond to the grace which is offered to save him from that state; when, far from avoiding occasions of sin he seeks them, or at least yields to them whenever they occur; when he hardly regards sin as an evil and never shuns the company of his worst enemy? Is it not a mockery to ask for deliverance from an evil that he does not fear, an evil that he loves and in which he finds pleasure? This nevertheless is the attitude of the majority of worldly Christians, who none the less recite the *Paternoster* every day, according to a habit formed in the days of their childhood, without thinking of what they are saying or applying the words to their present condition. God forbid that I should blame them for holding to such an excellent habit, but surely its first and least result should be their return to God and a prompt renunciation of sin.

As for those who consider small faults to be nothing at all, as being simply unpleasing to God and carrying no danger to their own salvation, we can only say that they deceive themselves on the latter point, and that they could not more openly insult him whom they call Father than by showing indifference to his displeasure, provided that there is no risk of eternal loss to themselves. Suppose a son who should have no respect for his father and would only obey him just so far as would save him from being disinherited, would he not have cause to be deeply ashamed of his conduct if he were capable of any thought or feeling at all? How could he avoid blaming himself in his heart for fulfilling the sacred duties laid upon him by nature, with no motive but his material interests and slavish fears? How much more is not a child of God to blame for acting on these same principles!

As for the evils of this present life, the Gospel teaches us that they are not strictly evils at all but may become very great blessings, if we regard them with the eyes of faith through the holy use made of them. Since Jesus Christ voluntarily endured the greatest of those evils, those from which nature shrinks the most, it is forbidden to his disciples to plead their natural aversion and to judge of the matter according to the flesh; especially when they remember that he took those evils upon him as a surety for us, making them serve to restore God's glory, to expiate our sins and to win for us the graces that preserve us from sin or take our sin away. The perfect Christian will not ask for deliverance from evils of this kind, but will rather pray that he may suffer them patiently, sanctifying himself by accepting them.

As for the imperfect Christians who make up far the greatest number, since they are not strong enough to draw spiritual profit from temporal afflictions, which provoke them to sin by arousing impatience, rebellious murmuring and despair; God is not displeased that they should pray to him to deliver them from such evils. He even responds to their faith and their prayers, and grants their requests for their greatest good, sometimes by means of miracles.

But he desires that the principal motive in our minds, when we thus pray for heavenly succour, should be to serve him with a freer spirit, with more love, gratitude and faithfulness. He desires us to feel humbled by the weakness that prevents us from profiting from these evils, and to pray for their removal, not in order to be relieved from suffering but because by our fault they hinder our salvation. Finally, he desires that we should make no comparison between these temporal evils and the true evil which is sin, and that we should be resolved to suffer such evils to the utmost rather than to be relieved of them at the expense of conscience. A man is not a Christian at all unless he thinks and acts in this way with regard to the sufferings and afflictions of this life.

Here let every man look into his heart and judge himself.

However wide my interpretation of the Lord's Prayer may have been, it seems to me that I have said nothing useless, nothing irrelevant to the subject. I have done nothing but develop the meaning contained in the words, neither have I any fear of being reproached for taking them in too lofty a sense, with perfection as the end in view. Without doubt, Our Lord intended to propose perfection to us in this prayer, and it would be blasphemous to think that the mind of man, even when enlightened from above, could add anything in this respect to the thought of Jesus Christ. We must always own that any explanation will always be less exalted than the meaning of words that come from divine lips.

Therefore, to pray this prayer well, to have in our hearts its sentiments and to follow them faithfully in our lives, is to be in the way of perfection.

Are we then in that way? I do not ask if we have made much progress in it, but only whether we have entered upon it, or at least wish to do and are striving to do, we who since our earliest years have recited the *Paternoster* several times a day. Let us examine ourselves in this matter and enquire into the sentiments of our hearts, with regard to each of the petitions that I have expounded. There is no more important enquiry, and that we may make it more thoroughly let us remember that we shall have for our judge him who has given us this prayer.

To put my own thought in a word, I am profoundly convinced that only the true children of God, only those who according to St. Paul are led by the spirit of God in all things and are submissive to the dominion of grace, ever repeat this prayer in a way that fully carries out the intention of Jesus Christ, and that in various degrees of perfection according to the progress they have made.